Thomas Cook **pocket** guides

SICILY

Your travelling companion since 1873

Written by Ryan Levitt and updated by Jo-Ann Titmarsh

Published by Thomas Cook Publishing
A division of Thomas Cook Tour Operations Limited
Company registration no. 3772199 England
The Thomas Cook Business Park, Unit 9, Coningsby Road,
Peterborough PE3 8SB, United Kingdom
Email: books@thomascook.com, Tel: + 44 (0) 1733 416477
www.thomascookpublishing.com

Produced by Cambridge Publishing Management Limited
Burr Elm Court, Main Street, Caldecote CB23 7NU

ISBN: 978-1-84848-253-1

First edition © 2008 Thomas Cook Publishing
This second edition © 2010
Text © Thomas Cook Publishing
Maps © Thomas Cook Publishing/PCGraphics (UK) Limited

Series Editor: Adam Royal
Production/DTP: Steven Collins

Printed and bound in Spain by GraphyCems

Front cover photography © foodfolio/Alamy

CONTENTS

INTRODUCTION.............................5
Getting to know Sicily.................8
The best of Sicily...........................10
Symbols key.....................................12

RESORTS.......................................13
Palermo...15
Cefalù...21
Letojanni...26
Mazzarò...28
Taormina...31
Giardini Naxos.................................36
Catania...41
Syracuse...49

EXCURSIONS..............................57
Monreale...58
Messina..61
Mount Etna..65
Forza d'Agrò & Savoca.................68
Agrigento..71
Marsala...74
Calatafimi-Segesta.........................77

LIFESTYLE....................................79
Food & drink.....................................80
Menu decoder...................................88
Shopping...91
Children...95
Sports & activities..........................98
Festivals & events..........................100

PRACTICAL INFORMATION.....103
Accommodation...............................104
Preparing to go...............................106
During your stay.............................111

INDEX..125

MAPS
Sicily...6
Palermo..14
Taormina...30
Catania...42
Syracuse...50
Messina..62
Agrigento..70

WHAT'S IN YOUR GUIDEBOOK?

Independent authors Impartial, up-to-date information from our travel experts who meticulously source local knowledge.

Experience Thomas Cook's 165 years in the travel industry and guidebook publishing enriches every word with expertise you can trust.

Travel know-how Thomas Cook has thousands of staff working around the globe, all living and breathing travel.

Editors Travel-publishing professionals, pulling everything together to craft a perfect blend of words, pictures, maps and design.

You, the traveller We deliver a practical, no-nonsense approach to information, geared to how you really use it.

ABOUT THE AUTHOR

Ryan Levitt is a travel writer and editor who has worked for some of the UK's leading magazines, newspapers and publishers including *The Independent on Sunday*, *Wallpaper*, *Arena*, *Jumeirah International*, *Cathay Pacific Inflight*, VisitBritain, The German National Tourist Office and many more. He has appeared on BBC Radio's *Traveller's Tree* as an expert discussing New York City.

● *Mazzarò beach near Taormina*

 # INTRODUCTION
Getting to know Sicily

Getting to know Sicily

The island of Sicily has been ruled by dozens of empires during its turbulent history, ever since the Greeks settled on it back in the 8th century BC. Before this time, legends told of monsters roaming the countryside ready to devour any who decided to test the gods by exploring its coveted coves and mountains. Since then, Roman, Phoenician, Arab, Norman and Spanish conquerors have fought over this precious Mediterranean jewel, eager to exploit its riches and agricultural bounty. The result is an ethnic, cultural and culinary mix that is incredibly diverse and well worth exploring.

Despite its attractions to the empires of yesteryear, Sicily never experienced a true peak, only really coming into its own under the leadership of the medieval Norman kings. However, once it lost its status as the base of this powerful regime to the city of Naples, it never truly recovered, eventually resulting in centuries of neglect as a backwater province.

A trip to Sicily can feel like a step back in time to the days when farming was done with a horse and cart, when strolling entertainers kept audiences enrapt and trading was done from market stalls.

By far the biggest city in Sicily is Palermo, capital of the island and home to the largest airport. While it isn't a popular beach resort, new low-cost flights from the UK have opened up this historic city as a potential sun-drenched weekend break perfect for culture vultures. Further east along the north coast is Cefalù, a popular resort due to its combination of great beaches and medieval architecture. The top sun destinations, however, can all be found along the east coast of the island. Depending on whether you prefer chic sophistication or action-packed locales chock-full of amenities, there is bound to be a resort for you along this stretch of coastline. For beach flopping, Letojanni and Mazzarò offer plenty of options. Taormina, meanwhile, is the choice for celebs despite its lack of beach access. Meanwhile, Giardini Naxos is the place to go if non-stop fun is what you desire.

Finally, there are the historic cities of Catania and Syracuse further south, and of course the volcanic action of Mount Etna (Europe's most active volcano), the Greek treasures of Agrigento, and the hilltop *Godfather* settings in Forza d'Agrò, where Al Pacino began his career as the king of the mafia dons.

⬥ *Typical housing in Cefalù*

THE BEST OF SICILY

Classical architecture, medieval streets to explore, golden-sand beaches... it's all here in Sicily. While the entire island greets you with beautiful views and experiences at every corner, some of the more unmissable attractions and things to do include:

TOP 10 ATTRACTIONS

- **Art in Palazzo Abatellis** Palermo's Galleria Regionale Siciliana provides the perfect backdrop to some of Italy's most serene art of a mostly sacred nature (see page 16).

- **Granitas at Bar Vitelli** Sit in the very location in the town of Savoca where Al Pacino, in his role as Michael Corleone in *The Godfather*, asks the patron for the hand in marriage of his daughter Apollonia (see page 69).

- **Trekking Etna** Feel the power of a planet boil under you as you hike up Europe's most active and volatile volcano, the great Mount Etna (see page 65).

- **Topping up the tan in Giardini Naxos** Catch some rays in Sicily's most action-packed and facilities-filled resort. Quiet and picturesque it might not be, but the proximity to Taormina and golden-sand beaches can't be beaten (see page 36).

- **Sunset strolling at Mazzarò** Join the chic set and stroll down the promenade in this seaside resort boasting easy access to the treasure that is Taormina (see page 28).

- **Monreale Cathedral** Norman architecture reached its peak in this cathedral, considered one of the finest examples of construction from the medieval age (see page 58).

- **Puppetry with Pinocchio** Join the kids in watching marionettes move – as if by magic (see page 97).

- **Syracuse's Greek Theatre** Sit down in the amphitheatre and watch some of the world's oldest plays performed in front of your very eyes (see page 51).

- **Getting lost in Taormina** For travellers on a European Grand Tour during the 19th century, a stop in Taormina was a society must. Drawn to the winding streets, delicate flower blossoms and classical architecture, travellers fell in love, many choosing never to leave again (see page 31).

- **Wander the ruins of the Valle dei Templi** This temple complex in Agrigento may be over 2,500 years old but it continues to inspire thanks to a combination of graceful lines and a superb natural setting (see page 73).

⬇ *Performances are still held in Syracuse's ancient Greek Theatre*

SYMBOLS KEY

The following symbols are used throughout this book:

ⓐ address ⓣ telephone ⓦ website address

ⓒ opening times ⓘ important

The following symbols are used on the maps:

𝒊	information office	○	city
✉	post office	○	large town
✈	airport	○	small town
✚	hospital	■	POI (point of interest)
🛡	police station	═	motorway
🚌	bus station	—	main road
🚆	railway station	=	minor road
✝	church	—	railway
❶	numbers denote featured cafés, restaurants & evening venues		

RESTAURANT CATEGORIES

The symbol after the name of each restaurant listed in this guide indicates the price of a typical three-course meal without drinks for one person:

£ = up to €15   ££ = €15–25   £££ = over €25

▶ *The beautiful Giardino Pubblico in Taormina*

 # RESORTS
Places under the sun

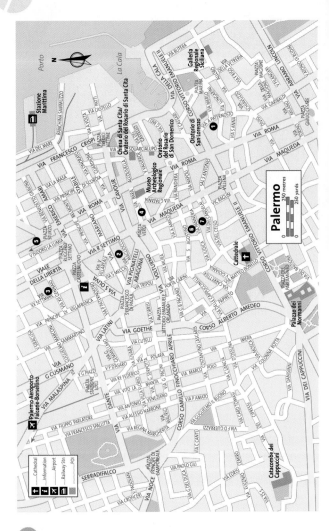

Palermo

For years, visitors to Sicily, in favour of the more notable ancient towns and sun resorts of the east coast, have avoided Palermo. Times change, however, and the introduction of low-cost flights to the city airport from the UK (and other European departure points) has opened up the option of visiting the city as a unique weekend break. To dismiss Palermo is to miss out on one of Italy's greatest capitals of culture, a metropolis packed with historical points of interest, incredible art galleries, intriguing neighbourhoods and fantastic food. As the crossroads of the island (which is, in turn, the crossroads of the Mediterranean), the Sicilian capital boasts a diverse population able to trace its heritage through the numerous empires that once based themselves in this great city.

While Palermo has been in decline for a number of years, its bad reputation is a relatively recent phenomenon due to its status as the mafia headquarters of the nation. Most tourists won't come into contact with this underbelly of society, but residents may be wary if you ask too many questions about this challenging societal problem.

To truly get in touch with Palermo, get your comfortable shoes on and start walking the neighbourhoods. Sicily is all about people and character, and nowhere else will you find a more welcoming bunch. In addition to the main sights listed in the following pages, a great route to consider is a wander through the La Kalsa district. Home to the poorest residents of the city, it's an atmospheric collection of crumbling *palazzi* and churches. Restoration is beginning to take place in the quarter, bringing money and artistry back where it belongs. Gentrification, however, is not complete, so be sure to keep hold of your belongings at all times and don't even think about wandering alone through La Kalsa's streets after dark.

THINGS TO SEE & DO

Catacombe dei Cappuccini (Catacombs of the Capuchins)

Over 8,000 Sicilians are buried in these catacombs under the Capuchin Monastery. By a fluke of nature, the catacombs feature a strange atmospheric anomaly that keeps bodies preserved for many years after death, resulting in the almost life-like appearance of many of the inhabitants.

ⓐ Piazza Cappuccini 1 ⓣ 091 212 633 ⓛ 08.30–13.00 & 14.30–18.00 ❶ Admission charge

Cattedrale (Cathedral)

The architecture of Palermo's cathedral is like a history lesson in a building. Every conquering empire has added a little something to the mix, resulting in a combination of styles ranging from Norman austerity to neoclassical splendour. While the result is intriguing at best, it is well worth visiting, if only to see the tombs of the Norman kings that made the city such a powerhouse during the medieval period, including that of Roger II, the first king of Sicily.

ⓐ Piazza di Cattedrale, Corso Vittorio Emanuele ⓣ 091 334 373 ⓛ 09.00–17.30 Mon–Sat ❶ Admission charge for crypts and treasury only

Chiesa di Santa Cita/Oratorio del Rosario di Santa Cita (Church of St Cita)

If you're short on time, choose to limit your visit to the oratory of Santa Cita; Allied bombing did much to destroy the bulk of the original church's beauty. Focus your attention on the magnificent baroque splendour of the oratory, and you'll be rewarded with the sight of all the cherubs, flowers and intricate detail you would expect from the period.

ⓐ Via Valverde 3 ⓣ 091 332 779 ⓛ 09.00–13.00 Mon–Sat ❶ Admission charge

Galleria Regionale Siciliana (Sicilian Regional Gallery)

This art gallery is probably the finest in southern Italy and a true must-see on any Sicilian itinerary. Housed in a converted *palazzo*, it boasts superb Flemish and Italian paintings, porcelain and sculpture.

ⓐ Via Alloro 4 ☎ 091 623 0062 ⏱ 09.00–13.30 Fri–Mon, 09.00–13.30 &
14.30–19.30 Tues–Thur ❗ Admission charge

Museo Archeologico Regionale (Regional Archaeological Museum)

If it was once buried or lost in Sicily, then chances are it has found its way
here. While archaeological museums exist throughout the island, this is
the mother of them all. Most digs will send their masterpieces to this
collection, leaving just a few minor finds for the regional counterparts.
The finds from Selinunte are a highlight to any visit here.

ⓐ Via Bara All'Olivella 24 ☎ 091 611 6806 ⏱ 08.30–18.15 Tues–Sat,
09.00–13.00 Sun ❗ Admission charge. Recently restored, some rooms
may be closed so call ahead for details

⬥ *Palermo skyline*

Oratorio del Rosario di San Domenico (Oratorio of St Dominic)

This 16th-century oratorio is notable for the works of two sculptors, Pietro Novelli and Giacomo Serpotta, who contributed dozens of marble and stucco works to the edifice, resulting in the outstanding interiors you see today.

ⓐ Via dei Bambinai ❶ 091 332 779 ❷ 09.00–13.00 Mon–Sat

Oratorio di San Lorenzo (Oratorio of St Lawrence)

Built by an order of Franciscans, this gorgeous church is famous for its stuccowork and for its beautiful pews inlaid with mother-of-pearl. Look closely to see the cheeky nudes frolicking with each other in the various panels; daring for its day.

ⓐ Via Immacolatella ❶ 091 611 8168 ❷ 10.00–18.00 daily

Palazzo dei Normanni (Norman Palace)

If you're only passing through Palermo and have time to see just one thing, then make it this palace, home to the ruling families of Sicily since the 9th century. Originally an Arab construction, it was built over a former Roman fortress and then restored by the Normans following their arrival and subsequent dismissal of Arab forces. Highlights to any visit include the Palatine Chapel with its mosaic-encrusted royal throne located at the entrance to the nave, the royal apartments and the Hall of Mirrors. Give yourself at least two hours to soak in all the sights.

ⓐ Piazza del Parlamento ❶ 091 705 1111 ❿ www.ars.sicilia.it
❷ 08.30–12.00 & 14.00–17.00 Mon–Sat, 08.30–12.30 Sun
❶ Admission charge

TAKING A BREAK

Antica Focacceria di San Francesco £ ❶ Great paninis and focaccia sandwiches for those days when another heaped bowl of pasta or a heavy fish dish doesn't suit your needs. ⓐ Via Alessandro Paternostro 58 ❶ 091 320 264 ❷ 12.00–15.00 & 18.30–22.00 Tues–Sun

◔ Palermo's Caffè Opera is a great spot for lunch

Pasticceria Mazzara £ ❷ Catch up on all the local gossip by standing at the espresso bar and ordering a caffeine-rich cup and pastry. ⓐ Via Generale Magliocco ❶ 091 321 443 ❶ 07.30–22.00

AFTER DARK

Restaurants & bars
Agricantus £ ❸ Great live music venue with an ever-changing repertoire of acts. ⓐ Via XX Settembre 82a ❶ 091 309 636 ⓦ www.agricantus.org ❶ 20.00–01.30 Tues–Sun

Pizzeria Italia £ ❹ For a light dinner, head over to Palermo's oldest pizzeria boasting fantastic thin-crust pizzas with every topping imaginable. ⓐ Via dell'Orologio 54 ❶ 091 589 885 ❶ 19.00–23.00

Villa Niscemi Pub £ ❺ Pavement tables, weekly live music sessions and late opening hours draw crowds of young locals to this always-jumping drinking den. There are even musical instruments available on-site if you have the nerve to join the entertainment. ⓐ Piazza Niscemi 55 ❶ 091 688 0820 ⓦ www.villaniscemipub.it ❶ 18.00–03.00, closed Mon

Il Firriato £££ ❻ Don't be surprised by the limited menu at this hotel restaurant located in the elegant Hotel Principe di Villafranca. The small selection ensures quality is maintained in every dish, especially for the dessert course. ⓐ Via G Turrisi Colonna 12 ❶ 091 612 4148 ❶ 12.00–14.30 & 19.00–22.30 Mon–Sat

Clubs
Candelai ££ ❼ Bop till you drop at this popular club that's always packed with Palermo's young and beautiful. Don't expect much in the way of cool club sounds; this is strictly a locale for eurotrash. ⓐ Via Candelai 63 ❶ 091 327 151 ❶ 20.00–late Fri–Sun (May–Oct), 20.00–late Tues–Sun (Nov–Apr) ❶ Admission charge for concerts

Cefalù

Each coast of Sicily has its main resort, and along the north, Cefalù certainly is it. If you're a fan of foreign films, you may find this former fishing community familiar, as it was the setting for the Oscar-winning film *Cinema Paradiso*. A stay in Cefalù combines both history and relaxation. A great beach on the Tyrrhenian coast draws the masses, while a small scattering of churches and museums is enough to satisfy even the most culturally snobbish. For the truly intrepid, look above the town to La Rocca, a large outcrop that looms over the medieval village and is well worth clambering up if you have a minimal level of physical fitness (and aren't scared of heights!). Due to constant raiding during the medieval period, residents of Cefalù lived on top of La Rocca for four centuries until the protection of King Roger II finally convinced them it was safe to return from their precarious position.

BEACHES

Due to Cefalù's proximity to Palermo, the beaches at this north-coast resort are almost permanently packed with both day-trippers from the Sicilian capital and foreign tourists. Despite this, it remains a great stretch of sand. However, you may want to rent chairs from one of the private lidos for greater comfort and privacy. On the main beach, chair rentals cost approximately €5, with umbrellas running an additional €3. To get away from the crowds, head over to the Spiaggia Attrezzata where you will find blue sea, gorgeous beaches and free showers. You'll find this small beach just off the Lungomare, but it, too, experiences big crowds, especially during the high season. West of town are additional options in the form of the Spiaggia Mazzaforno and Spiaggia Settefrati. Less picturesque than Cefalù's main crescent, these sunspots are a bit out-of-the-way and feature fewer facilities than the lidos of the main resort. No matter which beach you choose, remember that children need to be watched at all times as the crowds can easily confuse even the most mature little ones.

THINGS TO SEE & DO

Duomo (Cathedral)

This austere Norman cathedral is the focal point of town that confuses visitors due to its exterior architecture that looks more like a military base than a place of worship. King Roger II ordered the cathedral's construction to give thanks after surviving a massive storm just off the

● *Cefalù town*

coastline. An initial glance may fail to impress, especially if you have already visited the cathedrals in Palermo and Monreale, but deeper inspections inside will reveal stunning mosaics covering the apse and vault. Restoration is ongoing at Cefalù's cathedral, so opening hours vary wildly. Check in advance if there have been any alterations to their posted times.

ⓐ Piazza del Duomo ⓣ 0921 922 021 ⓛ 08.00–12.00 & 15.30–19.00 (summer); 08.00–12.00 & 15.30–17.00 (winter)

Museo Mandralisca (Mandralisca Museum)

This eclectic collection of artefacts is notable primarily for *Ritratto di un Uomo Ignoto* (*Portrait of an Unknown Man*), a masterpiece painted by Sicilian artist Antonello da Messina in 1465. Other items on display are less interesting; however, it makes for a nice diversion if you have time to kill.

ⓐ Via Mandralisca 13 ⓣ 0921 421 547 ⓛ 09.00–19.00 (June–July & Sept), 09.00–23.00 (Aug), 09.00–13.00 & 15.00–19.00 (Oct–May)
ⓘ Admission charge

La Rocca

It takes about an hour to climb this rock featuring some of the best views in all of Sicily. It may seem impossible on hot summer days, but there are plenty of diversions along the way, including an ancient temple dedicated to Diana and various fortifications built by the Arabs and Normans.

ⓐ Accesso alla Rocca ⓛ No set hours

TAKING A BREAK

Il Covo del Pirata £–££ This charming restaurant in the heart of Cefalù has panoramic sea views from its terrace. The menu focuses on fish, and there is a small, but exemplary, wine list. ⓐ Via Vittorio Emanuele 59 ⓣ 0921 922 249 ⓛ 12.00–15.15 & 18.45–23.00

◆ *View of Cefalù from La Rocca*

La Scoglio Ubriaco £–££ Go through the dark interior to find the staircase that leads down to the sun-drenched terrace precariously sitting over a series of sharp rocks. On hot days, the sea breezes will do as much to inspire as the tasty Sicilian treats on the menu. ⓐ Via Carlo Ortolani di Bordonaro 2–4 ⓣ 0921 423 370 ⓛ 12.00–14.30 & 19.00–23.30 (July–Aug); 12.00–14.30 & 19.00–23.30 Wed–Mon (Sept–June)

AFTER DARK

Restaurants & bars

Bip Bop Bar £ Blackpool-on-the-Med is what this English-style pub may feel like to visitors, but the lively action is sure to please those in search of more vigorous entertainment. ⓐ Via Nicola Botta 4 ⓣ 0921 923 972 ⓛ 19.30–02.00 (summer); 19.30–02.00 Wed–Mon (winter)

Kentia £–££ Vegetarians will rejoice at the sight of this establishment's daily fixed-price menu catering specifically for their needs. Fish-loving companions will appreciate the well-cooked catch of the day. ⓐ Via N. Botta 15 ⓣ 0921 423 801 ⓛ 12.00–15.00 & 19.30–23.00 (June–Sept); 19.30–23.00 Wed–Mon (Oct–May)

Ostaria del Duomo £–££ At first glance this eatery looks like a typical tourist trap, especially as its location right on the Piazza del Duomo is so prime. Luckily, the food is good and prices are reasonable, making it a true find for those who like convenient cuisine. ⓐ Via Seminario 5 ⓣ 0921 421 838 ⓦ www.ostariadelduomo.it ⓛ 12.00–23.00 daily

Letojanni

When it comes to selecting a resort along the east coast of Sicily, you may be in for a hard decision. While Giardini Naxos focuses on non-stop fun, Taormina is strictly for the highbrow and Mazzarò acts as a buffer between the two. Letojanni differs from all of the rest by giving a little of almost everything. It lacks any sights of historical interest, yet boasts more sand and better family-friendly options than the crowded beaches further to the south. If you plan on having tots in tow, Letojanni makes for a great getaway, although you will have to forgo a bit when it comes to charm and atmosphere. Large-scale resorts and widespread development are transforming this popular resort and it is no longer the secret find it used to be. Just 5 km (3 miles) north of Taormina proper, it makes for a popular day trip amongst residents looking to dip their toes without mixing with too many tourists.

BEACHES

The beaches of Letojanni are wider, more spacious, yet more developed than any of the other beaches along the coast. The resort beaches, which are located to the north of Mazzarò and Taormina, are ideal for families as they offer the same number of facilities as places like Giardini Naxos, yet also give visitors a bit more room to breathe. Letojanni's main beach is less popular than other locales primarily due to the fact that it is that little bit more isolated. Access to Taormina requires a car or public transport, meaning that fans of culture and sightseeing tend to choose other strips of sand that are more conveniently located near the main highlight spots along the coast. Beach clubs or resorts reserve most of the best sand, so payment of a fee may be required for your place in the sun.

TAKING A BREAK

Beach Club Paradise £–££ More a destination than an actual restaurant, this beach club is a great place at which to spend your day due to the on-site freshwater pool, private pebble beach and great open-air restaurant specialising in large platters of fresh seafood. The fact that there is a lifeguard watching over everything makes it an ideal rest stop for families, too. Dining at the restaurant requires payment of a one-off entrance fee of €10, which includes use of a *chaise* and umbrella.
ⓐ Via Lungomare ❶ 0942 369 44 Ⓦ www.paradisebeachclub.eu
Ⓛ 09.30–18.00 (end May–mid-Oct)

AFTER DARK

Nino £–££ You'd better be hungry when arriving at this fantastic Sicilian restaurant. Creative takes on local favourites are certain to make you salivate. Be sure to leave room for the delicious homemade *gelato*.
ⓐ Via Rizzo 29 ❶ 0942 361 47 Ⓛ 12.30–14.30 & 19.00–22.30 (June–Aug);
12.30–14.30 & 19.00–22.30 Wed–Mon (Sept–Nov & Mar–May)

⬥ A beach at Letojanni

Mazzarò

For those wanting to combine Sicilian culture with soaking in the sun, Mazzarò offers the best of both options. As the closest and most convenient beach to Taormina, it has long been popular with the international jet set despite its shingle beach and lack of high-end properties. Most visitors choose to base themselves at Taormina, only popping down when the call of the sea becomes too strong for them, but it is just as easy to do it the other way around. Divers, snorkellers and nature lovers will enjoy the offerings of Capo Sant'Andrea, a small island now run as a reserve by WWF. There are a number of dive centres offering both introductory courses and advanced dives to interested visitors at rates starting from €40 a dive. For those desiring sand rather than shingle, head to the left from the cable car station to hit the sands of Spisone just a ten-minute walk away.

BEACHES

The beach at Mazzarò is the main beach of choice both for those staying in the resort itself and for visitors based in Taormina due to the cable-car that runs between the two destinations. As such, it can get very crowded during the peak summer months when both culture vultures and sun worshippers collide in a seething mass of humanity. Avoid the masses by renting a deckchair and umbrella from one of the numerous touts that work the area. Daily rental of deckchairs is about €12 per couple. A more secluded cove exists at Isola Bella, situated to the right of the beach and around the cape. Walking takes just a few minutes, but renting a boat for the journey is a popular and much more scenic alternative. This cove is far from secret, however, and can be even busier than the main strip at the height of the season.

TAKING A BREAK

La Capinera £ Situated directly on the beach is this seasonal restaurant that has a great selection of antipasti and seafood dishes. Vegetarians will find themselves well catered for if they order multiple options from the selection of starters. The interior is also attractive for those days when the weather turns chilly or overcast. ⓐ Via Nazionale 177 ⓣ 0942 626 247 ⓦ www.ristorantelacapinera.com ⓛ 12.00–15.00 & 18.30–23.00 Tues–Sun

AFTER DARK

Restaurants
Ristorante Angelo a Mare – Il Delfino £–££ Just a couple of minutes away from the cable-car station lies this great eatery boasting a flower-strewn terrace and a menu of items inspired by the sea. While meat is available, stick to the seafood specialities to ensure a good night out. As it's so close to the beach, it's a great choice for diners on their way back to Taormina after a day in the sun. ⓐ Via Nazionale ⓣ 0942 230 04 ⓛ 12.00–15.00 & 18.00–23.00 ⓘ Closed Nov–Easter

⬥ *Mazzarò beach can get crowded in the summer*

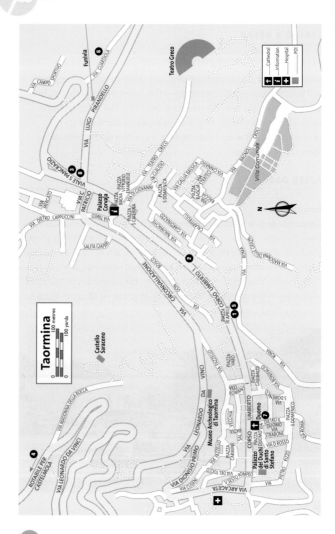

Taormina

Back in the days of the Grand Tour, a stop at Taormina was considered a must. The who's who of yesteryear were drawn to this sun-drenched resort due to its incredible views, precarious cliffside position, proximity to Mount Etna and romantic medieval atmosphere. The drawback to any stay in Taormina is its lack of a direct beach; however, the waterfronts of Giardini Naxos and Mazzarò are both an easy cable-car ride or drive away. Artists and writers have called Taormina home frequently during its past, including such notables as Tennessee Williams, Truman Capote, D H Lawrence and Goethe. Romantics will find themselves well catered for in the winding lanes of this town, while families and older travellers may prefer the convenience of the nearby beach towns, saving Taormina's charms for an easy day trip. To save money, try to avoid the high season between April and October when prices can as much as double.

THINGS TO SEE & DO

Duomo (Cathedral)

While it isn't the most decorative of cathedrals, its inspiration lies in its simplicity and relatively sparse façade. Built in the 13th century, the cathedral experienced numerous alterations during its history, with multiple additions occurring in the 17th century when a doorway and decorated windows were introduced. A number of worthy 15th-century sacred paintings are worth looking out for once inside, including a polyptych depicting the *Virgin Mary and Child* by Antonello Saliba. Be sure to take time out to enjoy the piazza immediately in front of the cathedral with its elegant baroque fountain.

ⓐ Piazza Duomo ❶ 0942 231 23 ❷ 08.30–12.00, 15.30–19.00

Museo Archeologico di Taormina (Archaeological Museum of Taormina)

During the Roman age, the grounds where this museum is situated housed the local baths. Most of the items on display are fragments of greater works discovered in the region, including a large collection of pottery shards.

ⓐ Via Circonvallazione ⓣ 0942 623 600 ⓛ 09.00–13.00 & 16.00–20.00 Tues–Sun ⓘ Admission charge. Closed for restoration, will reopen some time in 2010. Call ahead for details

Palazzo Corvaja

Explore the rooms of this 15th-century *palazzo* that once called itself home to Queen Blanche of Navarre and her royal court. Originally an Arab tower, it has since been 'Christianised' following additions of interior reliefs inspired by biblical scenes, and decorative details carved from the regional black lava stone.

ⓐ Piazza Vittorio Emanuele ⓣ 0942 232 43 ⓛ 08.30–14.00 & 16.00–20.00 Mon–Thur, 08.30–14.00 Fri ⓘ Admission charge

Palazzo dei Duchi di Santo Stefano (Palace of the Dukes of St Stephen)

This grand residence is a testament to the influence of Spanish rulers and Arab craftsmen. Once home to a family of Spanish dukes and princes, it features artistry constructed by master Arab craftsmen as showcased in the form of the black lava work on the exterior of the building.

ⓐ Via de Spuches ⓣ 0942 610 273 ⓛ 09.00–12.30 & 16.00–20.00 ⓘ Admission charge

Teatro Greco (Greek Theatre)

Probably the most beautiful theatre of all the amphitheatres in Sicily, this stunning performance space trumps all others due to its incredible natural backdrop. Both beaches at Giardini Naxos and mighty Mount Etna are in the background of the stage, which was originally carved from the side of a large hill. Alterations during the time of the Roman empire transformed the theatre into a gladiatorial space; however, elements of its original use as a theatrical space remain in the form of the various spaces and alcoves that lie among the columns backstage.

ⓐ Via Teatro Greco ⓣ 0942 232 20 ⓛ 09.00–1 hour before sunset ⓘ Admission charge

⬤ *Taormina's splendid amphitheatre is well worth visiting*

Villa Comunale

When you need a break from sightseeing, head over to this public garden packed with flora native to the region. The land was given to the town by a British noblewoman by the name of Florence Trevelyan, who fell in love with the town and spent much of her later years living in the area. If you're in search of shade, head over to the finely decorated tower for a brief respite in order to soak in the atmosphere and spot the various birds that call this green space home.

ⓐ Via Bagnoli Croci 🕐 07.00–24.00 (hours may vary)

TAKING A BREAK

Cafés

Café Wunderbar £ ❶ Hang with the bohemian crowd at this popular coffee bar perfect for an early-morning croissant or late-night caffeine jolt. ⓐ Piazza IX Aprile 7 🕿 0942 625 302 🕐 08.30–02.30 (Apr–Oct), 08.30–02.00 Wed–Mon (winter). Closed Jan

Pasticceria Gelateria Etna £ ❷ Satisfy your sweet tooth at this combination ice-cream shop/café/*pasticceria*. A great place to rest your feet. ⓐ Corso Umberto 112 🕿 0942 247 35 🕐 08.00–24.00

Porta Messina £ ❸ Tuck into one of the delicious pizzas at this simple eatery specialising in offbeat topping combinations. ⓐ Largo Giove Serapide 4 🕿 0942 232 05 🕐 12.00–15.00 & 18.30–22.30

AFTER DARK

Restaurants & bars

Bar San Giorgio £ ❹ Go to the top floor of the modern-looking café clinging precariously to a cliffside off the main square of Castelmola. The views from the glass-enclosed structure are superb, making it a great place to grab a coffee, light bite, or something a little stronger.

ⓐ Via Porta Mola 9, Castelmola 🕿 0942 282 28 🕐 07.30–24.00

Mocambo Bar £ **⑤** Located right on the main square, this popular bar is a great place for people-watching due to the pavement tables that allow wonderful views of the local citizens as they go about their business. Live music is played every evening to add to the ambience. ⓐ Piazza IX Aprile 8 ❶ 0942 233 50 ⏱ 08.00–02.00

La Piazzetta £–££ **⑥** Intimate and simple *trattoria* run by a family with a flair for fish. Dishes are typically Sicilian, never wavering too far away from the expected but always delicious. ⓐ Vicolo F. Paladini 5/7 ❶ 0942 626 317 ⏱ 19.30–24.00 Mon–Thur, 12.30–14.30 & 19.30–24.00 Fri–Sun (June–Sept); 19.30–24.00 Tues–Sun (Oct–May)

Casa Grugno £££ **⑦** The place to eat and be seen. The food comes from the gifted hands of resident chef Andreas Zangerl. His native Austria meets the shores of Sicily in the form of the pan-European menu featuring the finest ingredients available on the day. ⓐ Via Santa Maria de Greci ❶ 0942 212 08 ⏱ 19.30–22.30 Mon–Sat. Closed Jan–Feb

Clubs
Club Septimo £–££ **⑧** The eurotrash crowd congregates at this pumping nightclub boasting an amazing terrace and all the lighting effects and sound systems you could ever want. Music tends to be a mix of international and Italian club and pop hits. Dress to impress or reveal. ⓐ Via San Pancrazio 50 ❶ 0942 625 437 ⏱ 24.00–05.00 (June–Sept); 24.00–05.00 Sat (Oct–May)

Giardini Naxos

When mass tourism began to make Sicily more accessible to northern Europeans back during the 1950s and 1960s, visitors arrived at Taormina expecting a fantastic beach resort with plenty of local charm. They weren't disappointed by the charm, but they were surprised to see how difficult the seaside was to reach from the cliffside community. The result was the transformation of Giardini Naxos – a once quiet fishing community – into a modern tourist resort complete with all the bells and whistles one would expect from a full-service holiday destination. Concrete in appearance, it is a great place for families who want to combine sun and sand with cultural exploration in nearby Taormina.

Surprisingly, while Giardini Naxos is considered a modern creation, it's actually the oldest community on Sicily. Founded by the Greeks in the 8th century BC, it was the first permanent settlement on the island. However, little remains from this period with the exception of a few building foundations on the Capo Schiso.

BEACHES

The beach at Giardini Naxos became popular during the 1960s with the arrival of European package tourists who desired proximity to both the medieval streets of Taormina and an easily reachable beach. Almost all the hotels in the resort are located across the street from the golden sands. However, many feel that development has reached a point where the once pristine stretch of sand has become overrun. Where once there were quaint cafés and a vibrant fishing community, there are now souvenir shops, watersports centres, large-scale resorts and bustling *trattorie*. The main street running alongside the waterfront is the Via Schiso. Here is where you will find the bulk of the tourist-oriented establishments that cater to the vast numbers of visitors that descend on the beach every year.

Choose Giardini Naxos if you are looking for a resort that offers plenty of activities, easy access to the water and convenient proximity to

○ *Boats moored at Naxos beach*

Taormina with its medieval streets and classy charms. If somewhere quiet, romantic and intimate is more what you have in mind, choose a different resort.

THINGS TO SEE & DO

Archaeological Museum

The excavations at nearby Naxos dug up plenty of treasures and some of the best are kept at this small museum housed near a Bourbon-period keep. Artefacts on display include examples of pottery, statuettes and some intriguing medical items located in the tomb of an ancient surgeon. Items range from the Neolithic through Bronze Age eras and even feature a few nautical treasures such as anchor shafts and amphorae sourced from nearby shipwrecks.

ⓐ Via Schiso ⓣ 0942 510 01 ⓛ 09.00–19.00 ⓘ Admission charge

Excavations at Naxos

The Greeks first arrived on Sicily at this site on Capo Schiso (Cape Schiso) in 735 BC. Conquered, destroyed and rebuilt dozens of times since its initial founding, it is now a shadow of its former self thanks to generations of builders and archaeologists. What remain today are a few building foundations. The Greeks actually sailed past Sicily for many years before the community was founded, as legends of monsters dwelling on the land prevented anyone from attempting to approach. It wasn't until an Athenian by the name of Theocles was shipwrecked on the eastern coast that the discovery was made that the rumours were untrue. Settlers arrived shortly afterwards.

ⓐ Via Schiso ⓣ 0942 510 01 ⓛ 09.00–19.00

TAKING A BREAK

La Cambusa £–££ Great pizza joint located right by the oceanfront boasting incredible sea views. A great place for something cheap, cheerful and deliciously filling. At night, the menu and atmosphere

⬥ *Naxos excavations*

changes as torches are lit on the patio giving the eatery a romantic air. Also worth tucking into are the various pastas and tasty fish soup. ⓐ Via Schiso 3 ⓣ 0942 514 37 ⓛ 12.30–15.00 & 19.30–24.00; closed Nov–Mar & Tues (Sept–Oct & Apr–May)

AFTER DARK

Restaurants & bars

Lido da Angelo £–££ Sit yourself down at this restaurant directly over the beach and savour the food from the comfort of the choice balcony tables. Pizzas, pastas and fish dishes are all available, plus a great vegetarian antipasti buffet. Wash it down with a cold glass of local wine for an enjoyable lunch or casual dinner. ⓐ Piazza San Giovanni ⓣ 0942 519 02 ⓛ 12.30–15.00 & 19.00–23.00

Ristorante Sabbie d'Oro £–££ While it's technically a restaurant, this establishment situated under a pavilion feels more like an Italian pub due to the nautical (and slightly kitsch) items that decorate the ceiling and walls. While the food is passable, it's more the kind of place to grab a grappa at the end of a long day. ⓐ Via Schiso 12 ⓣ 0942 523 80 ⓛ 12.30–15.00 & 19.00–23.00. Closed Dec–Feb

Ristorante Sea Sound ££–£££ Located a little further away from the centre of town than other establishments, this restaurant doesn't feature the same welcoming charm as other eateries due to its concrete exterior, but makes up for it with a great terrace and wonderful antipasti and fish options. Meat dishes are less successful and can be hit-or-miss. ⓐ Via Jannuzzo 37A ⓣ 0942 543 30 ⓛ 12.30–14.30 & 19.00–23.30. Closed Nov–Mar

Catania

As the second-largest city in Sicily, Catania has always suffered a bit from little sibling syndrome. While Palermo gets all the glory, Catania sits and quietly suffers through the numerous disasters that have plagued its environs ever since it was founded back in 729 BC. The cause of its complaints is Mount Etna, Europe's most active volcano and a source of much annoyance to city residents. In the late 17th century, a massive eruption and a colossal earthquake did their best to erase the city from the map, only to see residents return and rebuild.

The bulk of Catania's treasures are constructed in the baroque style due to the massive restorations required during the period when this architectural style was at its peak. Intriguingly, black lava stone has been used in many buildings, highlighting Mount Etna's ever-looming presence.

Time has not been kind to Catania since its 17th-century heyday and many of the most important sights seem to be in various states of distress. What various earth rumblings and lava flows haven't affected, the Allied bombing raids of World War II did, resulting in the destruction of most of the city's most important historic sights. Despite this, there are still plenty of points of interest well worth examining, if only to see how a city at constant risk of natural disasters manages to survive.

As a university town, the nightlife of Catania is especially varied and lively. Opera is another passion among locals thanks to the beautiful opera house built in honour of noted composer Vincenzo Bellini, creator of the classic opera *Norma*.

Please note: Catania experiences a higher crime rate than all other Sicilian cities, especially after dark. Be aware of your surroundings and the people around you at all times and ensure your possessions are constantly guarded to avoid becoming victim to petty thieves.

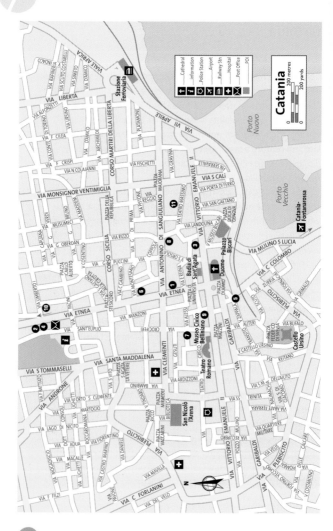

THINGS TO SEE & DO

Badia di Sant'Agata (Abbey of St Agatha)

Catania is filled with baroque architecture and this church provides one of the better examples in the form of its elaborate façade designed by Giovanni Battista Vaccarini. The rococo interior is also impressive, designed in the shape of an octagon.

ⓐ Via Vittorio Emanuele II ☎ 095 742 1111 🕐 07.30–12.00 Mon–Sat, 16.00–19.30 Sun

🔺 *Catania's cathedral was first built in the 12th century*

Castello Ursino (Ursino Castle)

The Aragonese kings once ruled Sicily from this castle overlooking the sea and built during the Middle Ages. As one of the few remaining examples of medieval architecture left in Catania, it is of interest both to castle fans and to those visiting the civic museum that lies on the upper floors. Look here for examples of sacred artwork created during the 16th century, the peak years of the castle's influence.

ⓐ Piazza Federico di Svevia ❶ 095 345 830 ⌚ 09.00–13.00 & 15.00–19.00 Mon–Sat, 09.00–13.00 Sun

Duomo (Cathedral)

Dedicated to the city's patron saint, St Agatha, this cathedral was originally constructed during the Norman reign. Subsequent construction transformed the façade into a baroque masterpiece. Go inside the right-hand transept after you enter to see the final resting place of countless Aragonese rulers.

ⓐ Piazza Duomo ❶ 095 320 044 ⌚ 07.00–12.00 & 16.00–19.00 Mon–Sat, 07.00–12.30 & 16.30–19.00 Sun

Museo Civico Belliniano (Bellini Civic Museum)

The childhood home of noted opera composer Bellini has been transformed into a museum chronicling his life and work. See maquettes from his operas, scores and personal letters in the various rooms that once housed the musical genius.

ⓐ Piazza San Francesco 3 ❶ 095 715 0535 ⌚ 09.00–13.00 Mon, Wed & Fri–Sun, 09.00–13.00 & 15.00–18.00 Tues & Thur

Palazzo Biscari (Biscari Palace)

Make an appointment to go inside this 18th-century *palazzo* built by Prince Paterno Castello. Construction took over a century to complete, with the most interesting façade visible on Via Dusmet.

ⓐ Via Museo Biscari ❶ 095 715 2508 ⓦ www.palazzobiscari.com
⌚ By appointment only

⬤ *Fontana dell'Elefante in Piazza Duomo*

Piazza Duomo (Cathedral Square)

This square is the traditional heart of Catania, lying at the junction of two of the busiest streets in town: the Via Etnea and Via Vittorio Emanuele. While in the square, take note of some of its treasures, including the Palazzo del Municipio (Town Hall), Duomo (cathedral) and the famed 18th-century fountain created by Giovanni Battista Vaccarini featuring an elephant made from black lava, called Fontana dell'Elefante (see page 45).

ⓐ Junction of Via Etnea and Via Vittorio Emanuele ⓛ 24 hours

San Nicolò l'Arena (St Nicolo l'Arena)

While this church is of interest architecturally, it is its possession of a splendid sundial that explains the crowds wandering about inside. Built during the 18th century after the destruction of a Benedictine monastery that existed on the same site until the earthquake of 1693, San Nicolò was intended to be the largest church in all of Sicily. While it never succeeded in fulfilling this mission, the sundial created in the mid-1800s is truly a work of both art and scientific accuracy.

ⓐ Piazza Dante ⓣ 095 312 366 ⓛ 09.00–13.00 daily ❶ The church roof is currently under restoration. Call ahead to check any variations in opening times

Teatro Romano (Roman Theatre)

Once one of the largest theatres in Sicily with a capacity to accommodate up to 7,000 audience members, this theatre suffered heavy damage in the 11th century when the Norman King Roger I permitted builders to strip the seating of its precious marble and limestone in order to construct the Duomo. While a theatre has existed on this site since the days of the Greeks, what remains is completely Roman in construction. A smaller odeon used for musical performances and competitions lies immediately next to the main amphitheatre.

ⓐ Via Vittorio Emanuele 226 ⓣ 095 715 0508 ⓛ 09.00–13.30 & 14.30–17.00 ❶ Admission charge

TAKING A BREAK

Café Charmant £ ❶ No matter what hour of the day, this classy café is sure to offer up something to sate your stomach or fill your caffeine quota. ⓐ Via Etnea 19–23 🕐 24 hrs

Caffè-Pasticceria Savia £ ❷ Over a century in operation, this café offers up great sweets, pastries and savoury snacks for both tourists and locals. Its location across from the Villa Bellini makes it a convenient rest stop. ⓐ Via Etnea 302–304 ☎ 095 316 919 🕐 07.00–21.00 Tues–Sun

La Marchesana £ ❸ During the summer months, the tables come out and fill the quiet street on which this friendly eatery is situated. Family-run, the establishment features menu items of both local favourites and recipes that have been kept secret by the owners for generations. ⓐ Via Mazza 6 ☎ 095 315 171 🕐 11.00–16.00 & 19.00–01.00

Spinella £ ❹ Best *pasticceria* in town due to the amazing quality of its *cannoli*. Service, on the other hand, is not too amazing. ⓐ Via Etnea 300 ☎ 095 327 247 🕐 07.00–21.00 Tues–Sun

Trattoria La Paglia £ ❺ In the heart of the fish market lies this unpretentious establishment serving... fish. Any kind you like, caught fresh on the day and picked up probably in one of the stalls nearby a few minutes ago. ⓐ Via Pardo 23 ☎ 095 346 838 🕐 12.00–15.30 & 19.30–24.00

AFTER DARK

Restaurants & bars

Joyce £ ❻ Wherever there are British and Irish travellers, there will always be an Irish pub and Catania's Joyce bar fits the bill nicely. Guinness® on tap and a courtyard make it a favoured home away from home. ⓐ Via Montesano 46 ⓣ 347 629 6930 ⓛ 21.00–02.00 Tues–Sun; closed mid-July–Aug

Nievski Pub £ ❼ Mix with Catania's bohemian set at this bar featuring Cuban revolutionary war posters and communist propaganda. ⓐ Scalinata Alessi 15 ⓣ 095 313 792 ⓛ 13.00–16.00 & 19.00–02.00

Ristorante al Piccolo Teatro £–££ ❽ This pub-style restaurant is popular with the after-work crowd due to the combination of rustic yet charming surroundings and tasty nibble-size treats. Pasta courses are especially recommended. ⓐ Via Michele Rapisardi 6–8 ⓣ 095 315 369 ⓛ 12.30–14.30 & 20.00–23.30 Wed–Mon

Osteria I Tre Bicchieri ££ ❾ If you're looking to make a meal of it, then make sure to do so at this beautiful restaurant that features the best selection of wines in Catania, if not all of Sicily. While the food is incredible, the interiors are even more inspiring, decorated authentically in the 18th-century style. ⓐ Via San Giuseppe al Duomo 31 ⓣ 095 715 3540 ⓦ www.osteriaitrebicchieri.it ⓛ 12.30–14.30 & 20.00–23.30 Mon–Sat

Il Canile £££ ❿ Traditional restaurant that serves up solid versions of Sicilian favourites. Dishes are simple yet well made. While a wow factor is missing, you can occasionally be bowled over if you order well on the day. ⓐ Villa del Bosco, Via del Bosco 62 ⓣ 095 733 5100 ⓛ 12.30–14.30 & 20.00–23.00

Clubs
Ixtlan £–££ ⓫ Highly regarded jazz club with regular jam sessions and live acts. ⓐ Via Teatro Massimo 33 ⓛ 18.00–02.00

Syracuse

During the days of the Greek empire, the city of Syracuse was one of the most important in the Western world. At its peak, the wealth and splendour of this ancient metropolis gave even Athens a run for its money and was a leading influence in Mediterranean trade and power for many centuries. Today, its former glory can be seen among the ruins of Ortygia, a small island joined by a single bridge to the mainland that holds most of the city's important historic sights. Here is also where you will find the best hotels and chic shopping. Be sure to stop in the Piazza del Duomo, considered one of the most beautiful public squares in Europe. Try to time your visit to enjoy the biennial Festival of Greek Theatre held in the amphitheatre every other June. It's one of the few remaining locations where you can see authentic performances of some of the world's most ancient plays.

BEACHES

Syracuse isn't known for its city beaches; murky waters, busy harbour traffic and rocky coastlines put off even the most intrepid swimmers. If a quick dip or sun soak is all you're after, book yourself a spot at the Lido Maniace (Ⓦ www.lidomaniace.it) close to the city centre. It may be a bit rocky and lacking in atmosphere, but it's a good place to rest if you're stuck in Syracuse.

Better beaches are easily accessible nearby if you don't mind driving or taking public transport. By far the best beach is Fontane Bianche, located 19 km (12 miles) to the south. You can reach it by driving along the SS115 or by taking bus number 21 or 22 from outside the central post office in Piazza delle Poste. Alternatively, if you don't want to go so far away, choose the Lido Arenella, which is about halfway along the same route and reachable using the same methods as it takes to get to the Fontane Bianche. It isn't as pleasant, but makes for a strong second choice in the event you need to stay within reach of town.

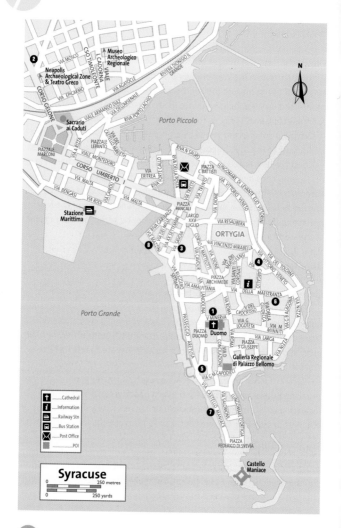

Syracuse

Cathedral
Information
Railway Stn
Bus Station
Post Office
POI

0   250 metres
0   250 yards

THINGS TO SEE & DO

Museo Archeologico Regionale (Regional Archaeological Museum)

It's hard to believe that this vast collection of ancient art has only been open to the public since 1988. All items on display were found in digs in the surrounding areas with treasures divided into three categories according to the period they hail from: prehistoric, Greek or post-Hellenistic.

ⓐ Parco Landolina, Viale Teocroto 66 ❶ 0931 464 022 ⏺ 09.00–1800 Tues–Sat, 09.00–13.00 Sun ❶ Admission charge

Neapolis Archaeological Zone

In order to make visiting easier, the archaeological highlights of the city have been grouped into a single area allowing tourists to pay one price for entrance. In addition to the Greek Theatre (see below), which deserves its own mention, the zone allows access to the stone quarries of Latomie, the Tomb of Archimedes and the Altar of Hieron II.

ⓐ Viale Paradiso ❶ 0931 662 06 ⏺ 09.00–15.00 (Nov–May); 09.00–18.00 (June–Oct) ❶ Admission charge

Teatro Greco (Greek Theatre)

Once one of the most important centres for theatrical production in the Western world, this enormous amphitheatre was the Royal Albert Hall of its day. While the structure seen today is impressive, it must have been even more inspiring before a significant portion of its stone was co-opted in order to construct the walls surrounding Ortygia in the 16th century. The theatre peaked in importance from the 5th century BC onwards when noted playwrights such as Aeschylus staged his tragedies on Syracuse's stage. It is possible to see the ancient Greek plays performed every other year during the biennial selection of productions put on in June by the National Institute of Ancient Drama.

ⓐ Viale Paradiso ❶ 0931 662 06 ⏺ 09.00–18.00 (Apr–Oct); 09.00–15.00 (Nov–Mar) ❶ Admission charge

● *Interior of Syracuse Cathedral*

Ortygia

The heart of Syracuse is on this island stronghold that separates the two harbours of the city. Linked to the mainland by the Umbertino bridge, this historically important pocket can trace its past back to the 6th century BC, as showcased by the Temple of Apollo, which greets all visitors when they come across from the mainland and enter the Piazza Pancali. Some of the highlights of a trip to Ortygia include the following:

Duomo (Cathedral)

Syracuse's cathedral was a relatively late addition to the city, built in the mid-18th century. The church is built over the top of an old temple honouring Minerva and actually includes elements of the temple, which dates back to the 6th century BC. Inside, keep a lookout for the beautiful Norman mosaics and 15th-century wooden choir stalls.

ⓐ Piazza Duomo ⓣ 0931 653 28 ⓛ 08.00–19.00

Galleria Regionale di Palazzo Bellomo (Bellomo Palace Regional Gallery)

Explore the history of Sicily through art by wandering along the halls as they take you through the various periods that have influenced Sicilian design and culture. Begin with a stroll past medieval and Renaissance sculpture and then pop upstairs to see the displays of Arabian and native ceramics, jewellery and paintings.

ⓐ Via Capodieci 16 ⓣ 0931 695 11 ⓛ 09.00–13.30 Mon–Sat, 09.00–12.30 Sun

TAKING A BREAK

Antico Caffè Minerva £ ❶ Whether you just need a cup of coffee or you're looking for a sweet treat, this café located close to the main cathedral is a lifesaver. Pull up a chair and watch the people go by as you relax in an oasis of elegance. ⓐ Via Minerva 15 ⓣ 0931 226 06 ⓛ 07.00–01.00 Thur–Tues

⬥ *Ortygia's backstreets*

Biblios Café £ ❷ Catch up with your communication by stopping off at this library/café/bookshop that's home to a number of local cultural institutions and clubs. An evening bar brings out the artsy set. ⓐ Via del Consiglio Regionale 11 ❶ 0931 214 91 ⓦ www.biblios-cafe.it ⓛ 10.00–13.30 & 17.00–21.00. Closed Wed am (& Sun July–Aug)

Il Mandarino £ ❸ Why this restaurant? Because it's one of the few offering decent non-Italian cuisine in Sicily. Don't just take a break from your day, give your palate a real treat by chomping down on the delicious Chinese dishes served up in classy surroundings. Large tables make it a good option for travelling families. ⓐ Via Savoia 12 ❶ 0931 228 98 ⓛ 11.00–15.00 & 18.00–24.00

La Baronie £–££ ❹ A meal at this place feels like a night dining with friends, the welcome is that warm. Simple Sicilian favourites are done very well at this unpretentious *trattoria*. Unknown to most tourists, it tends to draw a local crowd. ⓐ Via Gargallo 24 ❶ 0931 688 84 ⓛ 12.00–15.00 & 18.30–24.00 Tues–Sun

AFTER DARK

Restaurants & bars

Doctor Sam £ ❺ This bar pumps out hard music until the wee hours, drawing a who's who of Sicily's alternative set. Expect a lot of tattoos and piercings. ⓐ Piazza San Rocco 4 ❶ 0931 483 598 ⓛ 19.00–04.00; closed Wed (Oct–Mar)

Don Camillo ££ ❻ Fish fans rejoice! This eatery, constructed on the foundations of a 15th-century monastery that was destroyed during the 1693 earthquake, offers fantastic seafood, including sea urchins, an acquired taste if ever there was one. A fantastic wine cellar completes the perfection. ⓐ Via della Maestranza 96 ❶ 0931 671 33 ⓛ 12.30–14.30 & 19.30–22.30 Mon–Sat

Lungo la Notte ££ ❼ This picturesque restaurant specialises in fish dishes, as you'd expect from its location. Overlooking the city harbour, this is a popular haunt for locals and tourists alike. ⓐ Lungomare Alfeo 22 ⓣ 0931 642 06 ⓛ 11.30–01.30 daily

La Terrazza ££–£££ ❽ Formal elegance is the name of the game at this restaurant located in what is arguably the finest hotel on Ortygia Island. Courses offer slight twists and interesting flavours to common dishes, yet always boast the freshest of ingredients. ⓐ Grand Hotel, Viale Mazzini 12 ⓣ 0931 464 600 ⓦ www.grandhotelsr.it ⓛ 12.30–14.30 & 19.30–22.30

▶ *Climbing Mount Etna*

EXCURSIONS
Out & about

Monreale

This town of about 30,000 inhabitants makes for an easy day trip from Palermo. Although it offers stunning views of the bay (Conca d'Oro) from its hilltop perch, it would be of little interest to the average tourist if it weren't for the incredible 12th-century cathedral in the centre of town. The decision to build the cathedral was made by the Norman kings due to Monreale's location near the favoured hunting grounds of the royal family. Today considered by many to be one of the finest churches in Italy it is any visit's raison d'être and a must-see if you are in the region.

THINGS TO SEE & DO

Duomo di Monreale (Monreale Cathedral)

The cathedral in Monreale is truly the only reason to warrant a visit to this town, but what a visit it is. As a tourist attraction, the structure is certainly one of Sicily's best, regarded by many as one of the finest examples of Arab-Norman architecture ever created. The highlight to any visit is a glimpse of the incredible mosaics that cover the choir, transepts, nave and aisle depicting scenes from both the Old and New Testaments. Other things to check out include the outlook from the terraces offering incredible views over the cloisters – not recommended for those with mobility challenges due to the steep incline – and the inspiring bronze doors at the entrance to the cathedral designed by Bonnano Pisano, who also created the Leaning Tower of Pisa.

ⓐ Piazza Guglielmo il Buono ⓣ 091 640 4413 ⓛ 08.00–18.00 (May–Sept); 08.00–12.30 & 15.30–18.00 (Oct–Apr) ⓘ Admission charge

TAKING A BREAK

Bar Italia £ Popular during the mornings for its delectable coffee, biscuits and fresh croissants, this central bar is a good place to rest your

Architectural detail in the façade of Monreale's cathedral

feet.  Piazza Vittorio Emanuele 1 ❶ 091 640 2421 ❷ 05.00–22.00.
Closed Mon

Peppino £–££ Offering better quality than the bulk of the pizza and pasta
joints in this tourist town, Peppino is a good choice for solid Sicilian
cooking at a modest price. A little far away from the centre of town (four
blocks), it's worth the uphill walk. ⓐ Via B Civiletti 12 ❶ 091 640 7770
❷ 12.30–14.30 & 19.30–24.00 Fri–Wed

AFTER DARK

Restaurants
Taverna del Pavone £–££ Located on a cobblestoned square, this
delightful find is probably the best in town. The surroundings are rustic
and simple, yet the food is always fresh, using only locally grown
ingredients. Even the *gelato* is homemade. ⓐ Vico lo Pensato 18
❶ 091 640 6209 ⓦ www.tavernadelpavone.it ❷ 12.30–15.30 &
19.30–23.30 Tues–Sun

Messina

If you're arriving in Sicily by car, then chances are Messina will be your first port of call. Located just a quick ferry ride across the water from the Italian mainland, the city has traditionally been shunned by those driving through on their way to some of the more celebrated Sicilian towns and resorts. To ignore the place is to miss a location of extreme importance in Sicilian history, unique due to its long-standing tradition as a major crossroads for European, Mediterranean and Arabic cultures. While bombing raids during World War II almost flattened the city, it has since been rebuilt in a largely functional manner.

THINGS TO SEE & DO

Duomo (Cathedral)

What you see is not necessarily what you get at Messina's cathedral. Originally built between 1160 and 1197, the entire structure has practically been rebuilt in the modern day following massive destruction caused by the 1908 earthquake and World War II bombing raids. The result is a mix of architectural styles, with modern reconstructions mixed up with elements that were saved from the wreckage of the original church. Highlights include the central doorway, the Cappella del Sacramento (the last remaining mosaic retained from the original cathedral) and the gilt treasures of the Tesoro.

ⓐ Piazza del Duomo ⓣ 090 675 175 ⓛ 09.00–13.00 Mon–Sat (Oct–Apr); 09.00–13.00 & 16.00–18.30 Mon–Sat (May–Sept) ⓘ Admission charge

Museo Regionale (Regional Museum)

Regional museums focusing on the local history of a specific area are common in Italy. The collection boasts a wide range of notable pieces of art from the heyday of Messina between the 15th and 17th centuries. However, it is the chronicle of the 1908 earthquake that decimated the city that is of most interest, along with a fine pair of Caravaggio paintings created during his time in the city.

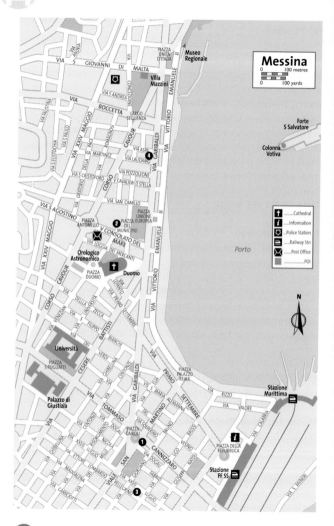

ⓐ Viale della Libertà ⓣ 090 361 292 ⓛ 09.00–13.30 & 16.00–18.30 Tues,
Thur & Sat, 09.00–12.30 Sun, Mon & Fri (June–Sept); 09.00–13.30 Mon &
Fri, 09.00–13.30 & 15.00–17.30 Tues, Thur & Sat, 09.00–12.30 Sun
(Oct–May) ⓘ Admission charge

Orologico Astronomico (Astronomical Clock)

Every day at exactly noon, this astronomical clock located in the bell-
tower of the cathedral whirrs into action to put on its daily show. Set to
the tune of Schubert's 'Ave Maria', it's an automated wonder complete
with flying banners, flapping chickens, bell ringing and even a figure of
Jesus at the moment of resurrection.

ⓐ Piazza del Duomo ⓛ Show daily at 12.00

⬤ Ferries in Messina harbour

TAKING A BREAK

Pasticceria Irrera £ ❶ Sit yourself down for some of Messina's best pastries and coffee for those times when you just need a break. On hot days the variously flavoured *granitas* (see page 90) are sure to quench your thirst. Of special delight are the items made from or including their famous almond paste. ⓐ Piazza Cairolli 12 ⓣ 090 673 823 ⓛ 08.00–20.30 Mon–Thur, 08.00–21.30 Fri–Sun

Le Due Sorrelle £–££ ❷ If you can snag a table at this tiny eatery, then this rustic restaurant is sure to offer plenty of menu items that will fill your stomach. Vegetarian dishes are especially good. At lunch, the place gets packed so it is best to drop in early. ⓐ Piazza del Municipio 4 ⓣ 090 447 20 ⓛ 13.00–15.00 & 20.00–24.00 Mon–Fri, 20.00–24.00 Sat & Sun; closed Aug

AFTER DARK

Restaurants & bars
The Duck £–££ ❸ Pub-style restaurant with a raucous clientele. Not the place to go if you're looking for something quiet. Solid meat and fish dishes prepared well are what draws the locals. ⓐ Via Ettore Lombardo Pellegrino 107A ⓣ 090 712 772 ⓛ 12.00–15.00 & 18.30–23.00 Mon–Sat

Jolly Restaurant dello Stretto ££ ❹ While the food is good, it's the views overlooking the marina that draw the crowds. Sure, the port is a bustling, modern monstrosity, but you can't help watch the buzzing ship traffic as you tuck into tasty versions of local specialities. ⓐ Jolly Hotel Messina, Via Garibaldi 126 ⓣ 090 363 860 ⓦ www.medeahotels.com ⓛ 13.00–14.30 & 20.00–22.30 ❶ Restaurant currently closed for restoration. Check ahead for details

Mount Etna

Looking for lava? Then you've come to the right place. Mount Etna is the largest, highest and most active volcano in Europe and, boy, is it active. Eruptions throughout the years have threatened Sicily's shores with black smoke and ash, yet it remains a much-loved (and feared) icon on the island. The most recent large-scale eruptions occurred in 2001 and 2002 when ash and smoke columns grew so thick that they could be seen from as far away as the coast of North Africa. In May 2008 there were significant eruptions with dramatic lava flow and fire fountains.

THINGS TO SEE & DO

Mount Etna

Ascending Mount Etna is a popular pastime, with two trails (a northern approach and a southern approach) available to volcano hunters. The northern route is generally regarded to be the more enjoyable of the two due to the cooler climate and more vibrant flora. The southern approach

◆ *Mount Etna*

◆ *Lava flow on Mount Etna*

rises along the route that most commonly experiences lava flows and is therefore much more sparse in terms of vegetation. Despite this fact, the southern route tends to see the bulk of the crowds as it is closer to Catania and more accessible as a day trip from this popular resort.

If you're expecting large-scale explosions and flames then you may be disappointed. At the smallest sign of activity, all bus tours are immediately cancelled and visitors are banned from getting near the top.

Etna Experience ⓐ Via Naumachia 103, Catania ⓣ 095 723 2924 ⓦ www.etnaexperience.com ⓛ Tours daily from 09.00. Minimum 4 people ⓘ Tour charge

TAKING A BREAK

Chalet delle Ginestre £–££ Take a drive to this modern chalet located 9 km (5½ miles) away from the motorway exit. For those undertaking a hike or trek up the mountain, this 'last-chance eatery' will fill you up. ⓐ Strada Mareneve, km10.8, Linguaglossa ⓣ 347 818 0990 ⓛ 12.30–16.00 (Oct–Feb); 12.30–16.00 & 20.00–22.00 (Mar–Sept); closed two weeks Nov

AFTER DARK

Restaurants

Ristorante Veneziano £–££ This sophisticated Sicilian establishment may lack rustic charm but more than makes up for it with its delicious menu of flavourful local delicacies. Meat dishes, including grilled steaks and homemade sausages, are especially tasty. ⓐ Contrada Arena, Randazzo ⓣ 095 799 1353 ⓦ www.ristoranteveneziano.it ⓛ 12.00–15.30 & 19.00–23.30 Tues–Sun

Villa Taverna £–££ Rustic décor will take you back in time to ye olde Catania at this evocative eatery specialising in Sicilian classics. ⓐ Corso Colombo 42, Trecastagni ⓣ 095 780 0716 ⓛ 12.00–14.30 & 19.30–23.00 daily

Forza d'Agrò & Savoca

For the real *Godfather* experience, avoid the town of Corleone and go instead to the glorious hilltop town of Forza d'Agrò to see where the film was actually shot. This medieval village stood in for Corleone after mafia bosses in Corleone prevented film-makers from arriving, fearful of the portrayal they were going to receive. Today, the town, along with the sister hamlet of Savoca, is packed with visitors looking to relive the film by retracing Al Pacino's steps through the village, before reaching Bar Vitelli for a drink in cinematic style.

THINGS TO SEE & DO

Castello Normano (Norman Castle)

Overshadowing the town of Forza d'Agrò is this 11th-century castle originally built by Count Ruggero. While the structure now lies in ruins, it

● *View up to Forza d'Agrò*

is an incredibly atmospheric place from which you can enjoy views of the town and nearby coastline. The journey to the castle is slightly precarious along a steep set of stairs built into a cliffside. Also of note are the remains of the Church of the Crucifix with its original bell-tower.

ⓐ Forza d'Agrò 🕒 No set hours

Convento dei Cappuccini (Capuchin Convent)

From the outside, you would never know that inside this pretty convent lies one of Sicily's most gruesome sights: a series of catacombs holding the bodies of 32 former townspeople who lived in the region between the 17th and 18th centuries. Depending on their class, they can be seen resting in splendour or simplicity.

ⓐ Piazza Cappuccini 1, Savoca 🕿 0942 761 245 🕒 09.00–13.00 & 16.00–19.00 (summer); 09.00–12.00 & 15.00–17.00 (winter)

TAKING A BREAK

Villa Souvenir £ This hotel, bar and restaurant complex is a good place to go for solid servings of traditional Sicilian fare. The pizzas are especially good, making this a great place for a lunch or light meal during your explorations. ⓐ Viale delle Rimembranze 13, Forza d'Agrò 🕿 0942 721 078 🅦 www.villasouvenir.com 🕒 12.00–15.00 & 20.00–24.00 (closed Thur winter)

AFTER DARK

Bars

Bar Vitelli £ In any other town, this bar would be just like any other, but Bar Vitelli is a star, famous due to its use as the location in *The Godfather* as the setting where Michael Corleone asks the father of his first wife for her hand in marriage. Also famous is the antique *granita* machine that produces probably the best ices in Italy during the hot summer months. ⓐ Savoca 🕒 12.00–22.00 ❶ Bar can close or become crowded during frequent coach tour visits

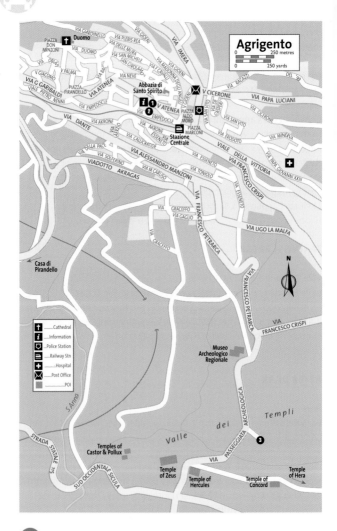

Agrigento

During the 5th century BC, the town of Agrigento (then known as Akragas) was one of the jewels in the crown of the Greek empire. Reflecting this prosperity was the construction of a vast number of temples lining a ridge near the modern-day community. Today, the complex provides some of the best examples of ancient architecture in Europe, despite numerous attempts during the Roman empire and Middle Ages to transform the complex into a quarry for the construction of local churches. Sunset provides the best viewing opportunities as the fading rays perfectly complement the limestone columns, imbuing them with a pink glow.

THINGS TO SEE & DO

Abbazia di Santo Spirito (Abbey of the Holy Spirit)
Desperately in need of restoration, this beautiful example of Gothic architecture boasts delightfully baroque interiors and high reliefs depicting key moments in the life of Christ. Be sure to purchase the chocolate and pistachio concoction made by the resident nuns as a sweet memento of your stay.

ⓐ Via Porcello/Via Santo Spirito 8 ⓣ 0922 490 011 ⓛ 09.00–13.00 & 15.00–17.30 Mon–Fri, 09.00–13.00 Sat & Sun

Casa di Pirandello (Pirandello's House)
Nobel Prize-winning author Luigi Pirandello called this building home, now littered with memorabilia chronicling his life. You'll find his burial spot under a pine tree in the grounds just a few hundred metres away from the house.

ⓐ Contrada Caos, SS115 ⓣ 0922 511 826 ⓦ www.pirandelloweb.com ⓛ 09.00–13.00 & 14.00–19.00 daily ⓘ Admission charge

Duomo (Cathedral)
It may once have been beautiful, but Agrigento's cathedral has been through a lot during its eight-plus centuries of existence. Built in the

12th century in the Norman style, this magnificent church features a beautifully painted ceiling and a letter from the Devil that was used to try to stain the purity of the local Virgin of Agrigento.

ⓐ Piazza Don Minzoni ☎ 0922 490 011 🕙 09.00–13.00 & 15.00–17.30 Mon–Fri, 09.00–13.00 Sat & Sun

Museo Archeologico Regionale (Regional Archaeological Museum)

This collection includes a number of artefacts dug up following the numerous excavations in the Agrigento region. The views of the Valley of the Temples are especially inspiring.

ⓐ Contrada San Nicola ☎ 0922 401 565 Ⓦ www.musei.it/sicilia/agrigento 🕙 09.00–19.00 Tues–Sat, 09.00–13.00 Sun & Mon
🅘 Admission charge. No photography allowed

⬤ *Ruins of Valle dei Templi*

Valle dei Templi (Valley of the Temples)

Immerse yourself in the beauty of the ancient world by visiting this collection of monuments housing a number of temples built by the Greeks in the 5th century BC and restored by the Romans four centuries later. Of the buildings, only one remains intact: the Temple of Concord. However, its conversion into a church in the 6th century resulted in numerous alterations. Highlights to any visit here include stops at the Temples of Zeus, Hercules, Castor and Pollux, and Hera.

ⓐ Valle dei Templi, Agrigento ⓣ 0922 401 565
ⓦ www.valleyofthetemples.com ⓛ 08.30–19.00 ⓘ Admission charge

TAKING A BREAK

Tempio di Vino £ ❶ Grab a crisp glass of cold white and rest your weary feet at this jazzy bar that also offers light antipasto plates to nibble on. ⓐ Piazza San Francesco ⓣ 0922 237 15 ⓛ 11.30–22.30 Mon–Sat

AFTER DARK

Restaurants & bars
Mojo Aperitif Wine Bar ££ ❷ Situated in the heart of town, this fun wine bar specialises in killer mojitos. Brimming with enthusiasm, the bar spills out into the square in summer and you can catch live music and other performances whilst downing your cocktail. ⓐ Piazza San Francesco 11-13-15 ⓣ 0922 463 013 ⓦ www.mojo4music.it ⓛ 19.00–03.00 Wed–Mon

Hotel Villa Athena ££–£££ ❸ Stuffy and pretentious this restaurant might be, but it also boasts an incredible atmosphere thanks to the stunning views (both by day and night) of the ruins of the Temple of Concord. ⓐ Via Passeggiata Archeologica 33 ⓣ 0922 596 288 ⓛ 12.30–14.30 & 19.30–21.30

EXCURSIONS

Marsala

If ever there was a town on Sicily where it could be said that Italy meets the Middle East, then Marsala would be it. Labyrinthine in layout, the streets wind around, end suddenly and are closely packed together much like an Arabian souk. World War II heavily damaged this port, so one can only imagine what evocative scenes played out in the city lanes before the bombs made their mark. Connoisseurs flock to Marsala to sample the sweet wines (similar to port) that are produced in the area. Be sure to sample a few varieties during your stay.

THINGS TO SEE & DO

Museo Archeologico di Baglio Anselmi
(Baglio Anselmi Archaeological Museum)
Another regional museum focusing on archaeological finds uncovered in the area. Pride of place goes to the reconstructed remains of a ship lost at the end of the First Punic War some time around 241 BC.
ⓐ Lungomare Boeo 32 ① 0923 952 535 ① 09.00–18.00 daily
ⓘ Admission charge

⬥ Visit a winery in Marsala for some tasting

Wine tastings

Wine is why the town of Marsala is so famous, so a stop at a winery should be considered a must if travelling through the region. Most tours will educate visitors on techniques and history with a tasting session organised at the end of the visit. Better vineyards to visit include:

Florio ⓐ Via Florio 1 ⓣ 0923 781 111 ⓦ www.cantineflorio.it
ⓛ By appointment only ⓘ Charge for tasting sessions
Pellegrino ⓐ Via del Fante 39 ⓣ 0923 719 911 ⓦ www.carlopellegrino.it
ⓛ By appointment only ⓘ Charge for tasting sessions

TAKING A BREAK

Ristorante Delfino £–££ This restaurant may not be the most convenient to reach, but a break here is well worth the effort due to its location right next to the seafront. Lap up the waves as you sup on the wide variety of fish on offer. The fish soups are particularly delicious. ⓐ Delfino Beach Hotel, Lungomare Mediterraneo 672 ⓣ 0923 751 011
ⓦ www.delfinobeach.com ⓛ 08.30–23.00; closed Tues Oct–Mar

AFTER DARK

Restaurants & bars

Divino Rosso £ Looking and feeling more like a wine bar, this establishment serves up delicious takes on Sicilian classic cuisine.
ⓐ Via XI Maggio 1 ⓣ 0923 711 770 ⓛ 19.00–24.00 Tues–Sun; closed Nov–Mar

Trattoria Garibaldi £–££ What makes this unpretentious eatery stand out is its extensive Sicilian wine list. Sip vintages from the region matched by great versions of favourite classics, including tasty pastas and antipasti. ⓐ Piazza dell'Addolorata 36 ⓣ 0923 953 006
ⓦ www.trattoriagaribaldi.com ⓛ 12.00–15.00 & 19.30–22.00 Mon–Fri, 19.30–22.00 Sat, 12.00–15.00 Sun

⬥ *The ancient Temple of Segesta*

Calatafimi-Segesta

Founded by the Greeks, Calatafimi-Segesta was a leading city in the Hellenistic empire during its heyday in the 5th century BC. Battles with its rival city Selinunte (Selinus) caused many skirmishes, eventually resulting in its destruction by the ruler of Syracuse who was allied with Calatafimi-Segesta's enemies. Today, a temple complex remains, considered by many to be one of the most perfect examples of architecture from the period due to an almost total lack of decay. Try to time your visit to coincide with the hour before sunset when the pale columns are bathed in a rosy glow, framing the rural views beyond.

THINGS TO SEE & DO

Teatro Greco (Greek Theatre)

Built at the top of Mount Barbaro in the 3rd century BC, this atmospheric theatre was carved directly out of the rock in order to accommodate audiences of up to 4,000. During the summer months, performances of both classical and modern plays are programmed every other year.

🄐 At the entrance to the Tempio di Segesta (see listing below)
🕒 Hours vary ❶ For performance schedules and tour information, contact the Temple of Segesta office (see below)

Tempio di Segesta (Temple of Segesta)

If you've seen a lot of temples, then you might be amazed to see how perfectly preserved the complex at Segesta truly is. Few crumbling columns or collapsed buildings are visible here. Instead, Segesta provides visitors with a true experience of what religious life and worship must have been like during the 5th century BC when the temple was created.

🄐 Segesta ❶ 0924 952 356 🕒 09.00–19.00 (summer), 09.00–18.00 (winter). Ticket office closes one hour before closing time
❶ Admission charge

TAKING A BREAK

There are no restaurants or cafés of quality to speak of in Calatafimi-Segesta. If you are planning a day trip, either come prepared with a picnic lunch or plan on a lunch-stop in Erice or Trapani, approximately 30 km (19 miles) away or 25 minutes by train, which runs ten times daily. The following listings are in Erice:

Pasticceria Michele Il Tulipano £ Have a quick drink at the stand-up coffee bar or tuck into a delicious pastry created on-site in this popular café that is always packed with locals. ⓐ Via Vittorio Emanuele 10–12 ⓣ 0923 869 672 ⓛ 07.30–21.00 (Sept–June); 07.30–02.00 (July & Aug)

AFTER DARK

Monte San Giuliano £–££ It can be hard finding this local favourite, buried within the winding streets of Erice, but the struggle is more than worth it in order to sample the fresh fish and local specialities featuring Arab influences. ⓐ Vicolo San Rocco 7 ⓣ 0923 869 595 ⓦ www.montesangiuliano.it ⓛ 12.15–14.45 & 19.30–22.00 Tues–Sun

◗ *Fishing boats in Mondello harbour, near Palermo*

 LIFESTYLE
The Sicilian way

Food & drink

EATING OUT

Sicily is an island that likes to enjoy its food – slowly. As such, service tends to be slow and you can expect to wait for a while between courses before the next item of food is set in front of you. While most restaurants do have menus, they often do not have English translations available, and restaurants that do have English versions tend to cater for tourists and are of lesser quality. Try to order one of the specials of the day to ensure your meal only uses the freshest of ingredients, usually purchased that very morning by the chef in the local markets.

Breakfast is a quick pastry or light bite, usually picked up over coffee on the way to work. Lunch is a more leisurely affair lasting a couple of hours between 13.00 and 15.00. Dinner is eaten late, often 21.00 or later, especially in the summer months.

ORIGINS

As Sicily has been conquered many times since it was first spotted by the Greeks, the cuisine of the island has developed and altered with each new regime change. The result is a surprisingly varied mix of flavours that differs wildly from the cuisine of the Italian mainland. Here, Arabic spices infiltrate the palate, citrus-based sauces are common, bluefish is prized highly and desserts are rich and creamy. Norman French meets North Africa on these shores and the results are always inspiring.

BREADS

When times got tough, bread was the only thing that kept many Sicilians alive. As such, it is greatly revered and served with almost every meal to make stomachs feel full longer. Local varieties are made from durum wheat and have a golden glow.

BREAKFAST

Breakfast is a simple affair, usually involving a cup of coffee and a fresh pastry or selection of breads. Local cafés generally have an ample supply

⬥ *Enjoy an evening meal outdoors in Taormina*

of freshly baked goods available for consumption, as residents often include a stop at their local coffee shop for a quick bite and a look at a newspaper on their way to work.

MAIN DISHES
Antipasti

Every Sicilian lunch and dinner starts with the antipasti course, a light serving of cheeses, marinated meats, fish and vegetables acting as a gentle kick-start to the stomach. Unlike their mainland counterparts, Sicilians won't serve large courses of antipasti, preferring instead to dive straight in to the pasta course. As such, there is little innovation with antipasti and main courses receive more of the glory when being written about in island cookbooks.

Pasta

A Sicilian staple, pasta is beloved by all residents as it's cheap and filling. By far the most common pasta versions on Sicily are *pasta a picchi pacchiu* (pasta with tomato and chilli sauce), *pasta alla Norma* (pasta in a rich ricotta and aubergine sauce) and *pasta con le sarde* (pasta with sardines). If you like Parmesan on your pasta, you may be out of luck as residents prefer topping their pasta dishes with *caciocavallo*, a strong cheese made from cow's milk.

Meat courses

Following pasta, a meat or fish course is served at Sicilian dinners. As expected, fish is favoured along the coast, while meat is the choice for those living inland. Beef, pork, rabbit and mutton are all commonly prepared, the most famous dish being *falsomagro*, an intricate dish of beef wrapped around sausages, boiled eggs, *prosciutto* and cheese cooked in a tomato sauce. The common rule-of-thumb in Sicily is that the higher into the mountains you go, the more frequently lamb and goat appear on the menu. Often, you will see the word *castrato* used to describe a dish. This means exactly what it looks like – the goat or lamb was castrated in order to prevent maturity and keep the meat tender.

🔺 *Fresh fish for sale*

Fish

As you would expect from a Mediterranean island, the favoured luxury of Sicilians is fish and seafood. No matter where you go on the island, you will be sure to find a plate of grilled fish waiting for you to enjoy at any hour of the day. Sicilian fishermen specialise in catching bluefish varieties, including tuna, mackerel and sardines. Swordfish is another favourite. Overfishing and a lack of conservation are beginning to affect fish stocks in and around Sicily, meaning that there are worries some varieties may soon no longer be on a menu near you.

Sicilian fish is prepared simply, usually grilled and lightly sauced with tomato or lemon-based toppings. Sweet-and-sour sauces are also favoured, with mixtures of tomatoes and raisins producing delightful combinations.

As a snack, baby squid is a popular choice, prepared in a variety of ways to pop into your mouth. Fried, stuffed or served in a tomato sauce, it all depends on your mood for the day.

DESSERTS

Sicilians have a sweet tooth and have concocted a number of desserts that are unique to the island. Locals have the Arabs to thank for the diversity of their sweet menu items as it was their conquering forces that introduced sugar cane to the region and the concept of frozen treats in the form of sorbets. From here it was only a matter of time before concoctions became even more extravagant as cheeses were sweetened, creams were added to the mix and the world was introduced to such gems as *gelato* and *panna*.

Desserts in Sicily tend to favour things such as sweet creams and cheeses or candied fruits rather than such recent innovations as chocolate. This is the Arab influence rearing its head again, as they introduced these preferred original flavours centuries ago in the form of fruits, sugars and flower waters. Strangely, Sicilians have Etna to thank for the innovation in frozen desserts, as it was the near-constant snows found on its peak that served to chill the sweet wines and ice creams developed by historical confectioners.

🔺 *Snails and fresh fruit for sale at Catania market*

The two most popular and well-known specialities are *cassata* (a dessert made from sweetened ricotta cheese, vanilla, candied fruits and chocolate) and *cannoli* (crisp, hollow tubes stuffed with sweet cream and candied fruits).

ALCOHOLIC BEVERAGES

Sicily is a major wine-producing region, famed for the quality of its vintages. The most notable wine of the lot is Marsala, a fortified wine made in the town of the same name along Sicily's west coast. Similar in taste to port or sherry, it boasts an alcohol content of 20 per cent and can vary in colour from amber to rich orange. Other wines to look out for include Malvasia wines from the volcanic island of Lipari, known for their strong bouquet, Faro red wines produced near Messina and served to accompany roast meats, and Moscata made from Muscat grapes and served as a dessert wine; spumante is the sparkling version of this variety.

There is no substantial local brewery; instead national brews are what's on offer, typically Peroni, Dreher and Moretti.

VEGETARIAN OPTIONS

Vegetables constitute a large bulk of the Sicilian diet, yet locals truly don't understand the concept of vegetarianism. During the island's turbulent history, famines and poverty were common, making meat a luxury item. Willingly choosing to refuse meat is therefore seen as a bizarre decision. This mentality means that menu items that look vegetarian may not be as meat-free as you might think. Many items that state that they are vegetarian involve meat stocks or *pancetta*. When in doubt, stick to pasta dishes and pizzas, but always be sure to ask your waiter for a full description of ingredients.

● *Palermo offers a wide range of outdoor cafés*

Menu decoder

MEATS, CHEESES & VEGETABLES

Abbacchio Roast lamb baked with an anchovy paste

Bocconcini Veal stuffed with ham and cheese, then fried

Braciola Pork chop

Caciocavallo Cheese made from cow's milk

Carciofi Artichokes

Costoletta alla siciliana Fried and breaded veal topped with garlic and Parmesan

Fagioli Beans

Fave Fava beans

Gorgonzola Strongly flavoured blue-veined cheese

Melanzane Aubergines

Mozzarella di bufala Unfermented cheese made from buffalo's milk

Osso buco Beef knuckle braised until tender

Pancetta Pork belly flavoured with herbs

Parmigiano Hard yellow cheese, often grated over soups or pastas

Peperoni Multicoloured sweet peppers

Piccata al Marsala Braised veal served in a Marsala sauce

Pizzaiola Beef in a tomato and oregano sauce

Ricotta Soft cheese made from cow's or sheep's milk

Saltimbocca Veal with *prosciutto* and sage

Scaloppine Veal, thinly sliced, coated in flour and fried

Stufato Braised beef in a white-wine sauce

Vitello tonnato Sliced veal served cold in a tuna sauce

SEAFOOD

Anguilla alla veneziana Eel cooked in a sauce made from lemons and tuna

Aragosta Lobster

Baccalà Stew made from salted codfish

Cacciucco ali livornese Seafood stew

Cozze Mussels

Fritto misto Seafood stir-fry, Italian-style

Involtini di pesce spada Grilled and breaded swordfish

Musseddu Salted and
fried tuna, often used
to give salads more
flavour

Pesce spada Swordfish

Polpetti Squid

Polpo Octopus

Seppia Cuttlefish

Sogliola Sole

Tonno Tuna

ANTIPASTI, SALAD & SOUP VARIETIES

Antipasti The first dish of
every meal, often consisting
of deli meats, marinated
vegetables or plates of
seafood

Bollito misto Boiled meats
of many varieties served
on a platter as an
appetiser

Carpaccio Raw beef cut into
thin slices and seasoned
with herbed olive oil

Insalata di frutti di mare
Seafood salad

Minestrone Vegetable soup
with grated Parmesan
cheese, often including
pasta

Zuppa di cozze Mussel soup

PASTA SAUCES & POLENTA VARIETIES

Gnocchi Potato or semolina
dumplings, usually in a
tomato sauce

Pansotti Pasta stuffed with
herbs and cheese with a
walnut sauce

Pappardelle alle lepre Pasta in
rabbit sauce

Pesto Green pasta sauce made
from pine nuts, basil,
cheese, garlic and olive oil

Polenta Cornmeal porridge

Polenta e coniglio Polenta
with rabbit stew

Polenta de uccelli Roasted
small birds served with
polenta

Ragu Tomato and meat mince
sauce (usually beef)

Salsa verde Green sauce made
from anchovies, lemon juice
and capers

Trenette Thin noodles served
with potatoes in a pesto
sauce

PIZZA VARIETIES

Calzone Stuffed pizza dough,
usually filled with ham and
cheese, and baked or fried

Capricciosa Black olives, ham and artichoke hearts

Margherita Pizza with tomatoes, mozzarella and basil

Napoletana Simple pizza with tomatoes, garlic, olive oil and oregano, and no cheese

Quattro Stagione 'Four seasons' pizza made from a choice of vegetables, bacon and ham

Siciliana Cheese, capers and black olives

SIDE DISHES

Arancini di riso Rice balls stuffed with either meat or cheese and then deep-fried

Bagna cauda Vegetable dip made from anchovies, always served hot

Frittata Italian-style omelette

Risotto Italian rice, often cooked in wine and mixed with seafood, meat or vegetables

DESSERT VARIETIES

Cannoli Hollow, crunchy pastry filled with sweet ricotta and a variety of other delights including candied fruit and chocolate

Cassata alla siciliana Layered dessert made from sponge, Marsala, sweet cheese and candied fruit topped with chocolate icing

Frutta candita Preserved fruit creation made from figs, oranges, tangerines and lemons

Gelato Ice cream

Granita Flavoured ice, often served with coffee

Panettone Sweet bread usually enjoyed with coffee

Panna Heavy cream

Semifreddo Literally 'semi-cold', a dessert served with ice cream and sponge

Zabaglione Whipped egg yolks flavoured with Marsala and served warm

Zuccotto Sponge soaked in liquor and layered with chocolate and nuts

Zuppa inglese Sponge soaked in custard, similar to English trifle

Shopping

The concept of shopping for pleasure is a relatively new one in Sicily because money has never really flowed across the island as freely as residents would have liked. While times have changed and Sicily is richer than it was, it still doesn't possess the buying power of somewhere like Milan or Rome. Locals will dress for function (older residents and grandmothers) or to show off their form (younger adults and teens), but high-end labels won't be flashed to all and sundry as often as you might see them on Capri or along the beaches of San Remo. What designer boutiques there are will be found in Palermo, which is also the city to go to if you need anything more than basics. Here is where you will find the best selection and most up-to-date styles. Stock is often limited in these boutiques and service may not always be with a smile. Most stock is locked away in drawers, so you will have to call on assistance at some point in time if you have plans to make a purchase.

If you aren't a fashionista, there are plenty of other wares to admire on the island, including jewellery, ceramics, wines and deli foods. Shopping in Sicily can sometimes feel like a step back in time as the concept of one-stop shopping continues to elude residents. If you need stationery, you will have to go to the *cartoleria* (stationery shop), and for medicines it's off to the *farmacia* (pharmacy). Every product is sold by a specialist seller, so general shops selling a variety of items aren't as common as you would find back home. If you really want to soak in 'real-life' Sicily, attend market day. Almost every town and village has a market day of some sort, always a good opportunity to make any regional food purchases that you are planning to bring back home. Just be aware that market food is fresh (no preservatives), and is likely to go off fast during a long journey.

SHOPPING AREAS

For high-end designer goods and local art galleries, do your shopping in Palermo. There are few boutiques supplying this kind of merchandise so when in doubt head to the city's branch of the department store La

◆ *Gourmet products make great souvenirs*

Rinascente for the basics. Ceramics, brought to Sicily by both Spanish and Arab conquerors, are produced throughout the island, with notable producers found in Sciacca, Caltagirone and Santo Stefano di Camastra. Gourmets won't want to miss stopping in Syracuse, Taormina and Cefalù, all widely acknowledged to offer the best deli options in Sicily. Sicilian wine is also a good purchase in these regions, unless you want the famous Marsala. For the best versions of this fortified variety, head to the town of the same name on the island's west coast. Alternatively, take a tour of one of the wineries and combine a tourist memory with a treasured purchase.

For jewellery, Trapani and Cefalù are the places to head for, especially if you're after gold, turquoise and coral pieces. Coral from Sciacca is particularly valued and worked into beautiful pieces in the jewellery shops of Messina, Syracuse and Taormina.

Finally, handmade lace is a favourite item to bring home. Find the best examples in the big cities of Palermo and Taormina.

MARKETS

Almost every town in Sicily has a market day or square, but the bulk of the items on offer is aimed purely at locals, consisting mostly of everyday household items or fresh foods such as cheeses, meats and sweets. For true variety, head to Palermo's Mercato della Vucciria, the best of the three markets in the island's capital. If you can't make it to Palermo, then the fruit and vegetable markets of Catania and Syracuse offer comparable experiences.

When shopping in the markets, be sure to keep your eye on your purchases and purses at all times, as the markets are often a prime location for pick-pocketing and petty theft. Also be aware that few stalls accept credit cards, so a supply of ready cash is advisable.

HANDICRAFTS & SOUVENIRS

The influences of the Spanish, Greeks, Normans and Arabs have given Sicily a rich cultural tradition to draw from throughout the years. This has translated into a large cottage industry of handicraft production ranging from ceramics and marionettes to embroidery and lace. Ceramic designs are heavily influenced by Arabian patterns, as it was the Arabs who originally brought ceramic production techniques to the island. Marionettes are popular due to their long-time use as actors in travelling plays telling the stories of the Middle Ages. And don't forget, the world's most famous puppet, Pinocchio, hails from these parts and is a frequently bought gift for children of all ages.

Long winters with nothing to do and no food on the table made the women of Sicily proficient lace-makers and embroiderers. The quality of the work is incredibly high, especially in the region of Erice. For something more specific to Sicily, consider purchasing a miniature version of a *carretti* (Sicilian handcart). These iconic carts, vividly painted in bright colours with bold shapes, were a common sight in Sicily for centuries, right up until the present day. They can be picked up in a multitude of sizes ranging from one small enough for your display cabinet to a large-scale one that can be used as a garden planter. There's nothing more distinctively Sicilian; it's guaranteed to bring back the holiday memories every time you see it.

🔺 *Fresh fruit and veg at Palermo market*

Children

ATTITUDES

Sicilians love children of every shape, size, variety and attitude. No matter how ill-tempered, fussy, noisy or active the child might be, a typical Sicilian will simply adore him or her.

Often, if you are with kids during your visit, you will be offered choice seats on public transportation and strangers will come up to ruffle the hair of your little one, especially if they have fair hair and blue eyes. Don't be offended or scared by these actions, as they are not intended to insult or frighten.

BEACHES

Beaches are the cheapest, easiest and fastest way to amuse kids of all ages. On those days when you can't face going to one more temple complex or walking up one more volcano, then head here. Sicily, after all, is an island and is ringed with sandy stretches of beautiful beach. Try to avoid city beaches as pollution levels can be high, especially near Palermo and Messina. Outside the main resorts, rocky outcrops can be common, lifeguards are few and the undertow is particularly strong, so be sure to either watch or accompany your little ones at all times.

MUSEUMS & HISTORIC SIGHTS

As an island boasting a long history, there are plenty of archaeological sights and museums worth exploring on Sicily. When travelling with kids, however, it is best to remember that one marble statue often looks exactly the same as all the others, so prepare your trip in advance by discussing Sicily's history and the differences between the sights in order to provide your child with an element of context before dragging them to the fifth temple complex of the day in blazing 40°C (104°F) heat.

The numerous museums and archaeological sites are naturally one of the draws of Sicily, and you would be well advised to carefully plan your sightseeing route in advance. A trip to Agrigento can be a nightmare, especially on hot days when the baking sun and lack of shade

⬥ *Ruins at Selinunte, south of Marsala*

can create havoc for families. Kids will find the ancient ruins fascinating for a while, but it would be advantageous for their patience levels and your state of mind to map your journey through the ruins in order to save time.

PUPPETRY

Puppetry is a tradition in Sicily and little kids love the shows put on for their pleasure. You don't always need Italian language skills to enjoy the fun or understand the story, as most fables presented are pretty universal in plot. For the best shows, head over to the Museo Internazionale delle Marionette in Palermo.

Museo Internazionale delle Marionette ⓐ Piazzetta Niscemi 5, Palermo
ⓣ 091 328 060 ⓛ Performance schedules vary according to season

🔺 *Traditional Sicilian puppets*

Sports & activities

Sicilians are ardent fans of watching sports, they just don't like playing them all that much. Perhaps it's the heat or the lack of facilities, but when it comes to working up a sweat, Sicilians would rather not. Looking good is a major influence in driving younger residents into the gyms and onto the beaches, but once locals hit 40, the inevitable middle-age spread tends to kick in and little is typically done to prevent it. Gyms are starting to become popular as residents become more aware of the importance of exercise in maintaining a healthy and long life, but these are primarily restricted to the larger cities. Health clubs are rare in Sicilian hotels, so stick to the nearby beach or on-site swimming pool to do your daily workout.

DIVING & SNORKELLING

Sicily's waters offer incredible diving opportunities, especially around the offshore Aeolian islands. A marine reserve exists around the island of Ustica, perfect for those looking for a serene dive surrounded by nature's underwater bounty. Most major resorts have a dive centre of some sort available to arrange trips. Be sure to check that dive centres are properly accredited, equipment is in good shape and staff are well trained, and ask other divers for tips and advice on which operator to go with before committing to anything.

FOOTBALL

While Sicilians love their footie, they have gone through many poor periods in the past. Recently, fortunes have been on the up, with two of the island's teams (Catania and Palermo) currently in the top tier of teams in Italy's premier league, the Serie A. Turin's Juventus also boasts a lot of support as many of Sicily's finest players were on their squad throughout the golden years of the 1960s–1990s. Palermo's La Favorita football stadium is the best place to catch a team in action; stands are always packed with ardent fans. Tickets are sold at news-stands in the city close to game time.

HIKING & TREKKING

Climbing Mount Etna is considered a must by active first-time visitors, drawn by the volcano's fame and the opportunities to see geological wonders happen before your eyes. Weather and seismic activity play a strong part in determining if a trek up is possible. For more details on Mount Etna, see page 65.

Other good walks and hikes to consider include the Madoni and Nebrodi mountain chains, and the limestone gorges of Pantalica. Most hikes or walks in Sicily are arranged through local tour operators. Planning your itinerary in advance can be a challenge due to the lack of information in international tourist offices. Once you reach your chosen resort, local tourist offices should be able to help.

SAILING

It may be the sport of the rich, but sailing is a popular pastime for Sicily's élite due to the island's strong maritime history. Ever since the America's Cup trials were held off the coast of Trapani in 2005, sailing has gone from strength to strength and it is possible to charter yachts of almost every shape and size for your personal needs. For details, check out the **Velalinks** website (Ⓦ www.velalinks.it) for details of charter operators on the island.

⬥ *Hiking in volcanic terrain*

Festivals & events

JANUARY

La Befana Celebrate the feast of La Befana in the town of Piana degli Akbanesi, near Palermo, on 6 January. Enjoy the colourful parade and fireworks showcase to mark the end of the Christmas season.

FEBRUARY

Carnevale Last chance to celebrate before Lent! Of the various parties during the week leading up to Lent, the celebrations in Taormina and Sciacca are most highly regarded.

Festa di Sant'Agata Catania comes alive during the annual procession when residents follow a silver reliquary through the city streets. 3–5 February.

Sagra del Mandorio in Fiore Held every year on the first Sunday in February, this folk festival brings live performances of dramatic and musical works to Agrigento.

○ *Sagra del Mandorio in Fiore, Agrigento*

MARCH/APRIL

Pasqua (Easter) Huge processions and passion plays dot the island. Trapani hosts the most internationally famous festival, known as *I Misteri*.

APRIL

Grand Prix Motor racing hits Sicily from the last weekend of April through October at the circuit in Lago di Pergusa, near Enna.

Settimana per la cultura For a single week in April, all the museums of Sicily are opened to the masses free of charge. ⓦ www.beniculturali.it

MAY

Beach Festival In the second week of May, head to Mondello (Palermo) to mix with other sun worshippers.

Inffiorata The town of Noto is festooned with blooms during its annual flower festival held annually on the third Sunday of May.

JUNE

Festival of Greek Classical Drama Witness authentic Greek Classical Drama during this festival held annually in Syracuse, home to the only school teaching the artform outside Athens. Variable dates.

Taormina Film Festival International event with screenings now shown in other parts of Sicily.

JULY

Festino di Santo Rosalia Celebrate the patron saint of Palermo, St Rosalia, 10–15 July. Probably the biggest party on the island all year.

AUGUST

Palio dei Normanni The town of Piazza Armerina recalls the day when the Norman King Roger I successfully kicked the Arabs off the island in this annual salute to the 11th-century battle, usually between 12 and 14 August.

Season of Food Festivals Various foodstuffs are celebrated through the months of August and September throughout Sicily, beginning with the Onion Festival on 15 August, Focaccia Festival in Chiaramonte, Fish Festival in Pozzallo, Grape Festival in Pedalino and Bread Festival in Monterosso Almo.

SEPTEMBER

Cous Cous Festival In the last week of September in San Vito Lo Capo, this festival is a must for lovers of Sicilian and North African cuisine.

Pelegrinaggi Pilgrimage month arrives with the pilgrimage from Palermo to Mount Pellegrino and the pilgrimage from Cefalù to the Madonie mountains occurring on 4 and 8 September respectively. Any and all are welcome!

NOVEMBER

Ognissanti A favourite with children, All Saints' Day is celebrated with children's toy fairs and the consumption of sickly-sweet sugar figures known as *pupe*, on 1 November.

DECEMBER

Festa di Santa Lucia Syracuse honours its patron saint, St Lucy, with processions and fireworks displays that light up the city on 13 December.

Natale (Christmas) The entire island gears up for Christmas weeks in advance with the display of Nativity scenes at almost every church and regular sacred music performances leading up to midnight Mass on Christmas Eve, 24 December.

⊙ *Typical road signs in Sicily*

PRACTICAL INFORMATION
Tips & advice

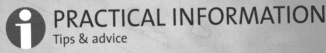

Accommodation

Price rating

Hotels in Italy are graded according to a star system running from 1-star for a cheap *pensione* to 5-stars for a luxurious resort with numerous facilities. The ratings below represent the average cost of a single night in a double room for two people, usually, but not always, with breakfast.

£ = under €100   ££ = €100–€200   £££ = over €200

PALERMO

Hotel Posta £–££ Clean, convenient and quiet, the three adjectives every good 3-star needs. ⓐ Via A. Gagini 77 ⓣ 091 587 338 ⓦ www.hotelpostapalermo.it

Grand Hotel Villa Igiea £££ Art nouveau splendour in the heart of Palermo. ⓐ Salita Belmonte 43 ⓣ 091 631 2141 ⓦ www.villaigieapalermo.com

CEFALÙ

Camping Costa Ponente £ Tent and caravan campsite with swimming pool and convenient beach access. ⓐ Contrada Ogliastrillo ⓣ 0921 420 085 ⓦ www.agricamping.it ⓛ Apr–Oct, closed Nov–Mar

La Giara ££ Renovated *pensione* in the heart of Cefalù. Some rooms feature terraces. ⓐ Via Veterani 40 ⓣ 0921 421 562 ⓦ www.hotel-lagiara.it

LETOJANNI

Villa Paradiso £££ This hotel isn't actually in Letojanni – it's in the romantic old town of Taormina nearby – but it's one of the few that offers free, direct shuttle service to the Paradise Beach Club in the heart of the resort. ⓐ Via Roma 2, Taormina ⓣ 0942 239 21 ⓦ www.hotelvillaparadisotaormina.com

MAZZARÒ

Grand Hotel Mazzarò Sea Palace £££ Modern, elegant property with great beach access and a private beach. The Hyd'Or Wellness Centre offers luxury spa treatments. ⓐ Via Nazionale 147 ⓣ 0942 240 04 ⓦ www.mazzaroseapalace.it

TAORMINA

Isoco Guesthouse £ An attractively furnished guesthouse offering an inexpensive alternative to hostels and campsites. ⓐ Via Salita Branco 2 ⓣ 0942 236 79 ⓦ www.isoco.it

Hotel del Corso ££–£££ Renovated 3-star property with good views in a resort not otherwise known for value. ⓐ Corso Umberto I 238 ⓣ 0942 628 698 ⓦ www.hoteldelcorsotaormina.com

GIARDINI NAXOS

Sant Alphio Garden Hotel ££ Glitz and glam or modern monstrosity – you decide at this, the largest property in Giardini Naxos. ⓐ Marina di Recanati ⓣ 0942 513 83 ⓦ www.santalphiohotel.com

CATANIA

Grand Hotel Baia Verde £££ Luxurious hotel with terraced rooms and stunning views of the Ionian. ⓐ Via Angelo Musco 8-10 ⓣ 095 491 522 ⓦ www.baiaverde.it

SYRACUSE

B&B Airone £ Backpacker and budget traveller favourite converted from a former *palazzo*. ⓐ Via Maestranza 111 ⓣ 093 169 005 ⓦ www.siracusahotel.com

Grand Hotel Villa Politi £££ Luxury, convenient access to the best archaeological sights and art nouveau architecture combine in this intimate, 100-room boutique property. ⓐ Via M. Politi 2 ⓣ 0931 412 121 ⓦ www.villapoliti.com

Preparing to go

GETTING THERE
By air

There are two main entry points to Sicily: Aeroporto Falcone-Borsellino serving the west of the island near Palermo, and Aeroporto Fontanarossa near Catania. Both are served by many major European airlines and some low-cost services. Travellers from the USA or Canada will need to change planes in a European hub before reaching their final destination, as there are no non-stop services. The following airlines fly to Sicily:

Alitalia ☎ 0870 000 0123 ⓦ www.alitalia.com
British Airways ☎ 0870 850 9850 ⓦ www.ba.com
easyJet ☎ 0871 244 2366 ⓦ www.easyjet.com
Fly Thomas Cook ⓦ book.flythomascook.com
Ryanair ⓦ www.ryanair.com

Many people are aware that air travel emits CO_2, which contributes to climate change. You may be interested in the possibility of lessening the environmental impact of your flight through the charity Climate Care, which offsets your CO_2 by funding environmental projects around the world. Visit ⓦ www.jpmorganclimatecare.com

By rail

Train services will only take you conveniently as far as Naples using the French routings from London's St Pancras International station with Eurostar. This involves a change in Paris, Turin and either Milan or Rome, ending at Villa San Giovanni, near Reggio di Calabria. The total journey time is approximately 30 hours depending on connections. The monthly *Thomas Cook European Rail Timetable* has up-to-date schedules for European international and domestic train services.

Eurostar ☎ 08705 186 186 ⓦ www.eurostar.com
Thomas Cook European Rail Timetable ☎ UK 01733 416 477, USA 1 800 322 3834 ⓦ www.thomascookpublishing.com

⬥ *Aerial view of Capo Passero Island, off Sicily's southernmost point*

By road

The Italian motorway system is well integrated in the European motorway network. Once in Italy, the easiest motorway to use is the A1, which cuts through the country and passes through Rome to terminate at Naples. The trip from London via northeastern France, Switzerland and along the Italian *autostrada* system, passing Florence and Rome, ends at Reggio di Calabria for the ferry to Messina. It's a long drive of approximately 20 hours.

By bus

Long-distance buses connect Sicily with most other European countries, but a ferry journey will be required at Reggio di Calabria to make the crossing to Messina. Most travellers will have to change coaches in an Italian city such as Rome or Naples for the final leg of their journey. From London by **National Express** (Ⓦ www.nationalexpress.com), the fastest journey time is about 24 hours to Naples followed by either a direct ferry from Naples to Palermo or onward coach services.

⬢ *Aeroporto Falcone-Borsellino*

TOURISM AUTHORITY

If you are in Sicily and need assistance or advice, there is a toll-free number accessible to visitors offering multilingual information on cultural activities, transportation, hotels and more.

Within Italy ☎ 800 117 700

From abroad ☎ 06 874 190 07

BEFORE YOU LEAVE
Health & prescriptions

Take regular prescription medicines with you to ensure you don't run out, and pack a small first-aid kit with plasters, antiseptic cream, travel sickness pills, insect repellent and bite-relief creams, upset stomach remedies, painkillers and protective sun creams. Most things can be bought easily at pharmacies, but communication can be a problem and rural areas are not so well equipped. Consider a dental check before you go if you are planning an extended stay in Italy. Ask your hotel receptionist or your tour operator rep to recommend a doctor or dentist in the event of an emergency.

Insurance

Check that your insurance policy covers you adequately for loss of possessions and valuables, for activities you might want to try – say horse-riding or watersports – and for emergency medical and dental treatment, including flights home, if required.

ENTRY FORMALITIES

Visitors to Italy who are citizens of the UK, Ireland, Australia, the USA, Canada or New Zealand will need a passport but not a visa for stays of up to three months. After that time they must apply for a *permesso di soggiorno* (permit to stay). If you are travelling from other countries, you may require a visa and it is best to check before you leave home.

MONEY

The currency in Italy is the euro. You can withdraw money using ATMs at many Italian banks. Bureaux de change are common, but commissions are equivalent to bank machines. Commissions depend on whether you are exchanging cash or traveller's cheques. Also, some offices charge a flat fee and offer a poor exchange rate, so ask what the deal is before exchanging anything to determine what works better for you. The most widely accepted credit cards are Visa and MasterCard. American Express is less commonly used.

CLIMATE

Sicily experiences a Mediterranean climate, which means it is hot, dry and bright during the summer and cool and damp during the winter. The temperature rarely drops below 0°C (32°F), but snow can be seen on Mount Etna during the winter months. Spring and autumn are considered the best times to visit, when temperatures remain moderate yet days are generally sunny.

BAGGAGE ALLOWANCE

Baggage allowances vary according to the airline, destination and the class of travel, but 20 kg (44 lb) per person is the norm for luggage that is carried in the hold. You are allowed one item of cabin baggage weighing no more than 5 kg (11 lb) and measuring 46 × 30 × 23 cm (18 × 12 × 9 in). Large items – surfboards, golf clubs and pushchairs – are usually charged as extras and it's worth notifying the airline in advance if you want to bring these. Be sure to limit your carry-on liquids as you can only take liquids on board in a small, clear, plastic bag with no more than 100 ml per container.

During your stay

AIRPORTS

The two largest airports on Sicily catering to international travellers are Aeroporto Falcone-Borsellino located 31 km (19 miles) west of Palermo, and Aeroporto Fontanarossa 7 km (4¹/₂ miles) south of Catania. No intercontinental flights land on Sicily, meaning that short-haul domestic and European traffic makes up the bulk of service, with the occasional charter servicing longer-haul destinations.

From Aeroporto Falcone-Borsellino, local buses ply the route to Piazza Giulio Cesare outside the main train station in Palermo. A one-way fare will cost you €6. If you choose to travel by taxi instead, keep an eye on the meter and be sure to follow the route the driver takes, as it is not uncommon for taxi drivers to confuse visitors by taking back routes to run up the fare. Count on the journey costing between €35 and €40. If driving in a rental car to town, it's a direct trip along the A29 *autostrada*. Depending on traffic, it should take you about 30 minutes to reach your destination. From the train station *piazza*, it is then possible to connect with inter-island train and bus services.

From Catania's airport, it's a quick 15-minute journey into town costing approximately €18. If you're on a budget, Alibus operates a regular service between 05.00 and 24.00 for just €1. Alternatively, those going straight on to Taormina can take a bus for about €5 one-way.

COMMUNICATIONS
Telephones

Italian phone numbers need to be dialled with their area codes regardless of where you are calling. Area codes vary according to what part of Sicily you are in, but numbers in Palermo will generally start with the code 091. Phone numbers in Sicily usually have seven digits. Older establishments may, however, have only six or even five. All numbers beginning with 800 are toll-free.

Public phones tend to be placed at busy intersections. As a result, it can be a challenge hearing anything that is being said down the line. The plus side is that almost everyone in Sicily has a mobile so public phone booths are almost always available. The minimum charge for a local call is €0.10. You will generally need a phone card to make calls. These are available from any of the numerous *tabaccherie*. Some public phones may also take credit cards, usually the phones at train stations and airports.

Italians love their mobiles (cellphones) and roaming services are pretty strong throughout the island. Rural areas and mountainsides are less well covered. Your mobile will have no problem working while you are in the country, but you should check charges with your local provider before making any calls.

TELEPHONING SICILY
The code for dialling Italy from abroad, after the access code (00 in most countries), is 39. To call Sicily from within Italy, dial the entire number including area code.

TELEPHONING ABROAD
When making an international call from Sicily, dial the international code you require and drop the initial zero of the area code you are ringing. Note the following international dialling codes for calls from Italy:

Australia **0061**
New Zealand **0064**
Republic of Ireland **00353**
South Africa **0027**
UK **0044**
USA and Canada **001**

For operator assistance within Italy, call 170.

Post

Italy's post system is beginning to improve after decades of unreliability. Post boxes are red and have two slots divided between local destinations (*per la città*) and everywhere else (*tutte le altre destinazioni*). Some also have a section with a blue sticker on the front for first-class post. For post being sent out of the country, first class is the only choice you have. First-class service promises 24-hour delivery for any destination in Italy, and three days for anywhere in the EU. For anywhere else on the planet, resort to prayer.

Letters weighing less than 20 g to Italy or other EU countries cost €0.65, or €0.82 to America. Australian post costs €1.20. Registered mail starts at €2.80.

Internet

Most Italian phone lines now have sockets for standard phone plugs (RJ11), although some you'll need an adapter for the power supply. Broadband in hotels is still a bit of a luxury, unless you are staying in a major-chain property. And you might as well keep dreaming if you yearn for wireless services. Internet cafés are scattered throughout the city and surrounding areas, each one varying in speed. Try to choose a business centre in a hotel or a café with multiple terminals to ensure high-quality service.

CUSTOMS

English is not commonly spoken in Sicily, especially in the smaller towns and villages, so a bit of advance preparation when trying to understand local customs is advised if you want to avoid offending residents. Have a look at the phrases on page 128 for help.

The entire region is incredibly superstitious, especially the older generation. If someone ever explains that you shouldn't do something because it attracts the 'evil eye', be sure to listen to them or they might think you are 'cursed'. Sundays are family day, so try not to make any plans with local friends unless it involves their inviting you to their weekly family gathering.

If you are using public transport or passing someone in the street, always give way to the elderly and mothers with children. Staying in your seat when a mother and child boards a bus is frowned upon heavily in these parts. And if you don't offer up to a black-clad grandmother, it could cause mass rioting.

When conversing, Sicilians are very animated, using wild gesticulations when both happy and sad. They may come up to you and invade your traditional sense of personal space, but this is not intended to threaten you (unless you happen to be in an argument). If you are having an argument, slowly back away, but if you back away during normal conversation, you could well offend someone, and this is the last thing you want to do, as tempers can flare hot and fast.

Service in shops and restaurants is very slow. In shops, most items are folded away in drawers while waiters may not approach you for days. This is not meant to annoy you; rather, locals look at eating and shopping as life's pleasures and prefer to extend the time in which both actions are done. For them, life is about quality rather than speed.

DRESS CODES

Shorts and T-shirts are absolutely fine when exploring Sicily, at least until night falls. The entire region is rather traditional and a bum bag strapped over jogging trousers or a cotton tee will immediately brand you as an uncouth tourist. For fine dining establishments (all day), or even when planning to check in to a 5-star hotel, it is advisable for you to prepare with light cotton or linen suits (for men) or summer dresses and blouses (for women). Around the beaches, skimpy beachwear and topless bathing is common, but you would be frowned upon if you decided to walk through the streets of Sicily in the same (lack of) attire. On Sundays in any town, a more modest dress sense is advised in order to respect religious sensibilities.

ELECTRICITY

The standard electrical current is 220V (50 hertz). Two-pin adaptors can be purchased at most electrical shops.

EMERGENCIES

Consulates & embassies

Australian Embassy ⓐ Via Antonio Bosio 5, Rome ☏ 06 852 721
Ⓦ www.italy.embassy.gov.au 🕒 09.00–17.00 Mon–Fri

British Embassy ⓐ Via XX Septembre 80, Rome ☏ 06 4220 0001
Ⓦ www.ukinitaly.fco.gov.uk 🕒 09.00–17.00 Mon–Fri

Canadian Embassy ⓐ Via Zara 30, Rome ☏ 06 8544 2911 Ⓦ www.canada.it

New Zealand Embassy ⓐ Via Clitunno 44, Rome ☏ 06 8537 501
Ⓦ www.nzembassy.com 🕒 08.30–17.00 Mon–Fri (Sept–June);
08.30–12.45 & 13.45–17.00 Mon–Thur, 08.00–12.30 Fri & 13.15–17.00
Mon–Thur (July & Aug); closed weekends

Republic of Ireland Embassy ⓐ Piazza di Campitelli 3, Rome ☏ 06 697
9121 Ⓦ www.embassyofireland.it 🕒 10.00–12.30 & 15.00–16.30 Mon–Fri

Republic of South Africa Embassy ⓐ Via Tanaro 14, Rome ☏ 06 852 541
Ⓦ www.sudafrica.it 🕒 08.30–12.00 Mon–Fri

US Embassy ⓐ Via Vittorio Veneto 119A, Rome ☏ 06 467 41
Ⓦ www.usembassy.it 🕒 08.30–12.30 Mon–Fri

EMERGENCY NUMBERS
Ambulance ☏ 118
Car breakdown ☏ 116
Carabineri (national/military police) ☏ 112
Fire brigade ☏ 115
Polizia di Stato (national police) ☏ 113

A scooter is one way to get about town

Medical services

If you need medical care during your stay, check the local English Yellow Pages, which lists English-speaking practitioners. Otherwise, your hotel and/or the local tourist office should have a list of possibilities. For serious emergencies, go directly to the emergency departments of any urban hospital, where English will be widely spoken.

Pharmacies (or *farmacie*) are marked by a green cross. Most pharmacies keep standard business hours (08.30–13.00 & 16.00–20.00 Mon–Fri, 08.30–13.00 Sat). It is the law that a sign needs to be posted by the front door pointing customers to the nearest late-opening pharmacy.

Police

Crimes can be reported to either the Carabineri or Commissariati. Don't hold your breath if you are looking to have something investigated fast, as any encounter is likely to frustrate. For your local station, call the emergency number, 112.

GETTING AROUND

Sicily is one of the better destinations to get around in terms of public transport. If you don't drive there is no need to fret as the extensive system of buses and trains that operate on the island is bound to get you to your final destination, even if you do need to transfer or have lots of patience in order to do it.

City buses

If travelling locally, city bus services are frequent and very efficient. Bus tickets must always be purchased prior to boarding and vary in cost depending on what town you're in. You must always validate your ticket when you board, but many locals ignore these warnings due to a shortage of ticket collectors. Palermo and Catania also boast limited metro systems that cater mostly to locals. They are primarily routes bringing workers into the city from residential neighbourhoods, meaning you are unlikely to require them at any time. Once again, tickets need to be purchased in advance and validated on boarding. Both bus and train tickets can be purchased at news kiosks or *tabacchi*.

Intercity buses

Longer-distance coach services are provided by a number of different companies and cater to both travellers looking to hop between major towns and those striving to reach more obscure towns and hamlets. If the location you are trying to get to is not near a major train line, then buses will be your only alternative. For bus timetables, ask at the city tourist offices or see if your required coach operator has a ticket office in town. At smaller villages, ask at the local bars, kiosks or *tabacchi* for information. Two large companies to consider are **SAIS Autolinee** (📞 091 616 602 28 or 800 211 020 🌐 www.saisautolinee.it) and **Interbus** (📞 093 556 5111 🌐 www.interbus.it).

Trains

Surprisingly, Sicily has an extensive network of train routes. These are operated by Trenitalia (📞 848 888 088 🌐 www.trenitalia.it). When in doubt, try to select Intercity (IC) trains for your journey, as these will be the fastest, stopping only at major cities. Anything other than an Intercity train will stop frequently, adding minutes (if not hours) to your travel time. In order of speed from fastest to slowest, trains are marked as *diretto*, *interregionale* and *espresso*. The worst of the lot are *regionale* trains, which will stop at any location that once housed a hut or small goat. Train fans should also take note of the **Ferrovia Circumetnea** (📞 095 541 111 🌐 www.circumetnea.it), a private train that performs an enjoyable circuit of Mount Etna.

Car hire

While public transport is extensive in Sicily and well run, the convenience of having your own wheels is enticing. The exception to this rule is if you are staying in Taormina, as a lack of parking and inconvenient access to nearby beaches makes driving obsolete. Locals are notoriously bad drivers and fender-benders are common.

◯ Take the Circumetnea train for a trip around Mount Etna

Consider renting a scooter, but be warned that accident rates on scooters are much higher. The minimum age for renting an economy car is 21 and you will need to bring your UK driving licence with you.

For a larger-cylinder car, you'll need to be 25. Most rental companies will require you to be covered for both theft and collision damage. If they don't, get it anyway. Local and international rental companies include:

Avis ❶ 800 331 1212 Ⓦ www.avis.com

Budget ❶ 095 536 927 Ⓦ www.budget.co.uk

easyCar.com ❶ 0906 333 333 3 (UK only) Ⓦ www.easycar.com

Hertz ❶ 800 654 3131 Ⓦ www.hertz.com

HEALTH, SAFETY & CRIME

It is not necessary to take any special health precautions while travelling in Italy. Tap water is safe to drink, but do not drink any water from surrounding lakes or rivers as the region is not known for its commitment towards environmentalism. Many Italians prefer bottled mineral water, especially sparkling varieties.

As the region is quite arid and hilly, hiking is a popular pastime. If you do decide to go for a stroll, it is best to inform someone before you embark on your journey as conditions can change fast, especially at the top of Etna. Be aware that signs will be posted on days when a climb up Etna is not permitted. DO NOT ignore these warnings as they may be related to seismic activity that could make you ill, if not kill you. Heatstroke is also a common problem so don't go anywhere without appropriate clothing and ample water supplies. Many visitors experience heatstroke when exploring historic sites of interest, such as Agrigento, due to the lack of shade, so a hat and plenty of sunscreen are vital.

Farmacie (pharmacies) are marked by a large green cross. Italian pharmacists can provide informal medical advice on simple ailments, but prescriptions will always cost more than they would back home.

Italian healthcare is of a good standard, but it is not free. In most cases your travel insurance should provide the coverage you need. Do not forget your EHIC (European Health Insurance Card), which will give you reduced-cost or, in some cases, free medical treatment.

Crime has long been a problem in Sicily (especially in Catania, Messina and Palermo). Its reputation is, however, far worse than reality. Petty theft (bag-snatching, pick-pocketing) is the most common form of trouble for tourists and activity is particularly high in the much-frequented historic sights and near the train stations and ferry ports. You are unlikely to experience violence or assault, which occur mainly in the context of gangland activities. Don't carry too much cash and try not to walk around late at night on badly lit streets (especially if you are a woman). Your hotel will warn you about particular areas to avoid.

When using public transport or walking on the street, carry your wallet in your front pocket, keep bags closed at all times, never leave valuables on the ground when you are seated at a table, and always wear camera bags and purses crossed over your chest. Police are easy to spot in their blue outfits with white hats, but there may not be as many on the streets as you would like. Additionally, many police officers do not speak English so you may have to go back with them to the station in order to report a crime.

MEDIA
Newspapers

The main English-language publications are international ones, available at newsstands in Palermo, Catania, Messina and Taormina. Kiosks in Palermo and Catania receive British newspapers and the *International Herald Tribune* either the same day or a day after publication in the UK. Kiosks in the major resorts may have a longer delay. Magazines are also readily available and tend to be either very news-orientated (*The Economist*, *Time*) or high on fashion and celebrity (*Vogue*, *OK!*, *Heat*).

Television

If staying at a hotel with satellite or cable, the two English-language stations you will get access to are BBC World and CNN.

Radio

Three state-owned stations – similar in output to the BBC stations of the UK – play easy-listening, jazz and classical music and provide regular news updates in Italian.

OPENING HOURS

Most **businesses** open 09.00–18.00 Mon–Fri, and many close for large chunks of the month of August, except in the peak tourist resorts near Taormina. **Retail shops** stay open until 20.00 with a two- to three-hour lunch break starting around 13.30. **Restaurants and cafés** usually close between lunch and dinner sittings from 15.30 until 19.00. Most also remain closed for breakfast. **Banks** open 08.20–13.20 & 14.45–15.45 Mon–Fri. **Cultural institutions** usually close for one day per week, usually Monday or Tuesday. Only the biggest and most popular sights remain open seven days a week. Sundays will, however, have limited hours. Usual **post office** opening hours are 08.15–19.00 Mon–Fri, 08.15–12.00 Sat.

RELIGION

While Italians are not extremely religious and going to Mass is becoming a less frequent ritual for the younger generation, Sicily remains fiercely Roman Catholic. This is especially true around the feast days of the various patron saints of the resort communities. Sunday remains an important family day, with many businesses shutting up shop even during the height of the season.

TIME DIFFERENCES

Italian clocks follow Central European Time (CET). During Daylight Saving Time (end Mar–end Oct) the clocks are put ahead one hour. In the Italian summer, at 12.00 noon, times elsewhere are as follows:

Australia Eastern Standard Time 20.00, Central Standard Time 19.30, Western Standard Time 18.00
New Zealand 22.00
South Africa 12.00

UK & Republic of Ireland 11.00
USA & Canada Newfoundland Time 07.30, Atlantic Canada Time 07.00, Eastern Standard Time 06.00, Central Time 05.00, Mountain Time 04.00, Pacific Time 03.00, Alaska 02.00

TIPPING

Tipping is not obligatory in Sicily, with the exception of some of the better restaurants, where 10 per cent is expected. If a service charge is included on your receipt, you will not be expected to add any more on top. Chambermaids and porters should be given about a euro a day, while taxi drivers will appreciate it if you round your fare up to the nearest euro.

TOILETS

There are very few public toilet facilities anywhere in Sicily. The best approach is to use the toilet in a bar. You can usually walk straight in without having to buy a drink. If the bar is empty, it is a matter of politeness to ask the bartender first. In restaurants there may be signs saying that toilets are only for use by paying customers. Fast-food joints and department stores are other good options.

TRAVELLERS WITH DISABILITIES

For people with disabilities, Sicily is a notoriously difficult destination to negotiate around. The best thing to do is to ask someone who works at the location you are trying to enter if they can help you, as there may be ramps that can be placed over stairs. In museums the ground floors are usually accessible, as are those in more modern galleries. Buses and trains, however, are completely wheelchair unfriendly. The following websites offer advice and information:

Ⓦ www.sath.org (US-based site)
Ⓦ www.access-able.com (general advice on worldwide travel)

◔ Rainbow over historic Taormina with Mount Etna in the background

A

accommodation 104–5
Agrigento 71–3
air travel 106, 111
architecture 16, 32, 41, 43–4, 58, 71–2, 77

B

baggage allowances 110
Bar Vitelli 69
beaches 21, 26, 28, 36, 38, 49, 95
buses 108, 111, 117–18

C

Calatafimi-Segesta 77–8
car hire 118, 120
Castello Normano (Forza d'Agrò) 68–9
Castello Ursino 44
catacombs 16, 69
Catania 41–8
Cefalù 21–5
children 26, 95–7
churches and cathedrals
    Abbazia di Santo Spirito 71
    Badia di Sant'Agata 43
    Cattedrale (Palermo) 16
    Duomo (Agrigento) 71–2
    Duomo (Catania) 44
    Duomo (Cefalù) 22–3
    Duomo (Messina) 61
    Duomo (Syracuse) 53
    Duomo (Taormina) 31
    Duomo di Monreale 58
    Oratorio del Rosario di San
        Domenico 18
    Oratorio del Rosario di Santa Cita
        16
    Oratorio di San Lorenzo 18
    San Nicolò l'Arena 46
climate 110
crime 15, 41, 117, 121

D

disabilities 123
diving 28, 98
driving 108, 111, 118, 120

E

emergencies 115, 117
etiquette 95, 113–14
events 49, 51, 77, 100–2

F

Fontane Bianche 49
food and drink 80–90, 93
    eating out 80, 82, 86 see also
        individual locations
    ice cream 84
    menus 88–90
    water 120
    wine 75, 86, 93
football 98
Forza d'Agrò 68–9

G

Giardini Naxos 36–40

H

health 109, 117, 120–1
hiking 65, 67, 99

I

insurance 109, 120–1
internet 113
Isola Bella 28

L

Letojanni 26–7
Lido Arenella 49

M

Marsala 74–5
Mazzarò 28–9
Messina 61–4
money 110
Monreale 58–60
Mount Etna 41, 65–7
museums and galleries 95–7
    Archaeological Museum (Giardini
        Naxos) 38
    Casa di Pirandello 71
    Galleria Regionale di Palazzo
        Bellomo 53

Galleria Regionale Siciliana
    16–17
Museo Archeologico di Baglio
    Anselmi 74
Museo Archeologico Regionale
    (Agrigento) 72
Museo Archeologico Regionale
    (Palermo) 17
Museo Archeologico Regionale
    (Syracuse) 51
Museo Archeologico di Taormina
    31–2
Museo Civico Belliniano 44
Museo Internazionale delle
    Marionette 97
Museo Mandralisca 23
Museo Regionale (Messina) 61, 63

N
Neapolis Archaeological Zone 51
newspapers 121
nightlife 20, 35, 47–8

O
opening hours 122
Orologico Astronomico (Messina) 63
Ortygia 49, 53

P
Palazzo Biscari 44
Palazzo Corvaja 32
Palazzo dei Duchi di Santo Stefano
    32
Palazzo dei Normanni 18
Palermo 14–20
passports and visas 109
phones 111, 112
police 117, 121
post 113
puppets 94, 97

R
radio 122
religion 122

S
safety and security 15, 41, 65, 67, 95,
    109, 120–1
sailing 99
Savoca 68, 69
shopping 91–4, 114
    carretti 94
    ceramics 93–4
    fashion 91
    food and drink 93
    jewellery 93
    lace 93–4
    markets 91, 93
    puppets 94
snorkelling 98
Spiaggia Attrezzata 21
Spiaggia Mazzaforno 21
Spiaggia Settefrati 21
sports and activities 28, 98–9
Syracuse 49–56

T
Taormina 30–5
taxis 111
Teatro Greco (Segesta) 77
Teatro Greco (Syracuse) 51
Teatro Greco (Taormina) 32
Teatro Romano (Catania) 46
television 121
Tempio di Segesta 77
time differences 122–3
tipping 123
toilets 123
tourist information 109
trains 106, 118

V
Valle dei Templi 73
Villa Comunale (Taormina) 34

NOWLEDGEMENTS

e publishers would like to thank the following for providing their pyright photographs for this book: Francesco Allegretto pages 22, 66, 96; nni Arponen/BigStockPhoto page 99; Diego Barucco/Dreamstime.com pages 10, 52; Reinhard Dietrich page 119; Bensliman Hassan/Dreamstime.com page 1; Charles Mahaux/Tips Images page 79; Ollirg/Dreamstime.com page 65; Marcella Pedone/Tips Images page 100; Pictures Colour Library pages 19, 27, 81, 83, 92, 116, 124; Guido Alberto Rossi/Tips Images page 107; Bernard J. Scheuvens/Wikimedia Commons page 108; Willy Vendeville/ Dreamstime.com page 9; Wikimedia Commons page 5; World Pictures/ Photoshot pages 37; Walter Zerla/Tips Images page 97; all the rest Mark Bassett

Project editor: Catherine Burch
Layout: Paul Queripel
Proofreader: Jan McCann
Indexer: Karolin Thomas

Send your thoughts to
books@thomascook.com

- Found a beach bar, peaceful stretch of sand or must-see sight that we don't feature?
- Like to tip us off about any information that needs a little updating?
- Want to tell us what you love about this handy little guidebook and more importantly how we can make it even handier?

Then here's your chance to tell all! Send us ideas, discoveries and recommendations today and then look out for your valuable input in the next edition of this title.

Email to the above address or write to:
pocket guides Series Editor, Thomas Cook Publishing, PO Box 227, Coningsby Road, Peterborough PE3 8SB, UK.

Useful phrases

English	Italian	Approx pronunciation
BASICS		
Yes	Sì	*See*
No	No	*Noh*
Please	Per favore	*Pehr fahvohreh*
Thank you	Grazie	*Grahtsyeh*
Hello	Buongiorno/Ciao	*Bwonjohrnoh/Chow*
Goodbye	Arrivederci/Ciao	*Ahreevehderchee/Chow*
Excuse me	Scusi	*Skoozee*
Sorry	Mi dispiace	*Mee deespyahcheh*
That's okay	Va bene	*Vah behneh*
I don't speak Italian	Non parlo italiano	*Non pahrloh eetahlyahnoh*
Do you speak English?	Parla inglese?	*Pahrlah eenglehzeh?*
Good morning	Buongiorno	*Bwonjohrnoh*
Good afternoon	Buon pomeriggio	*Bwon pohmehreejoh*
Good evening	Buona sera	*Bwonah sehrah*
Goodnight	Buona notte	*Bwonah nohteh*
My name is ...	Mi chiamo ...	*Mee kyahmoh ...*
NUMBERS		
One	Uno	*Oonoh*
Two	Due	*Dooeh*
Three	Tre	*Treh*
Four	Quattro	*Kwahttroh*
Five	Cinque	*Cheenkweh*
Six	Sei	*Say*
Seven	Sette	*Sehteh*
Eight	Otto	*Ohtoh*
Nine	Nove	*Nohveh*
Ten	Dieci	*Dyehchee*
Twenty	Venti	*Ventee*
Fifty	Cinquanta	*Cheenkwahntah*
One hundred	Cento	*Chentoh*
SIGNS & NOTICES		
Airport	Aeroporto	*Ahehrohpohrtoh*
Railway station	Stazione ferroviaria	*Statsyoneh fehrohveeahreeyah*
Platform	Binario	*Beenahreeyoh*
Smoking/non-smoking	Fumatori/non fumatori	*Foomahtohree/non foomahtohree*
Toilets	Bagni	*Bahnyee*
Ladies/Gentlemen	Signore/Signori	*Seenyoreh/Seenyohree*
Subway	Metropolitana	*Mehtrohpohleetahnah*